ChileGlobal Seminars UK

2013 – 2014

Edited by Elizabeth Wagemann, Bernardita Devilat, Dana Brablec, Marcos Stuardo and Cristian Soza

Editors
Elizabeth Wagemann
Bernardita Devilat
Dana Brablec
Marcos Stuardo
Cristian Soza

Graphic Design
Elizabeth Wagemann

ISBN: 978-956-358-346-5

Published by ChileGlobal Seminars UK

chileglobalseminarsuk@gmail.com
Twitter: @ChileSeminarsUK
Facebook:https://www.facebook.com/UKChileGlobalSeminars

Website:
http://www.chileglobal.net/categoria/chileglobal-seminars/
http://comunidad.chileglobal.net/seminars/londres/

This publication has been made possible with the financial support of ChileGlobal

CONTENTS

INTRODUCTION

ChileGlobal Seminars UK is a series of seminars organised by Chileans studying and/or working in the UK with the support of ChileGlobal and the Embassy of Chile. The aim of these seminars is to discuss, disseminate and share what is being researched about Chile in the United Kingdom and the impact of this for the country. The seminars are organised with the collaboration of the Chilean Societies of UCL, LSE and Manchester universities, the SEARCH Society and Red ICE.

Each seminar has a specific topic according to the abstracts received as contributions. The organizing committee selects the contributions according to the relevance for the seminar series objectives and the possible link to other presentations. The number and subject areas of abstracts received determine the topic of the next seminars, which will be coordinated with the already available calendar. We encourage you to send your work or to propose a session in a theme that is related to Chile. We are also open to the inclusion of guest speakers from other countries that can relate their work to the topic of each seminar, depending also on their availability.

ChileGlobal Seminars UK es una serie de seminarios organizados en conjunto por chilenos estudiando y/o trabajando en el Reino Unido, con el financiamiento de ChileGlobal y la Embajada de Chile en Londres. El objetivo de estos seminarios es discutir, difundir y compartir lo que se está investigando sobre Chile en el Reino Unido y el impacto de esto para el país. Los seminarios son organizados en colaboración con las Sociedades chilenas de las universidades UCL, LSE y Manchester, SEARCH Society y la Red ICE.

Cada seminario tiene un tema específico de acuerdo a los abstracts recibidos. El comité organizador selecciona las contribuciones de acuerdo a la relevancia que tenga para el objetivo de los seminarios y la relación que pueda tener con otras presentaciones. La cantidad y áreas de los abstracts recibidos determinará el tema de los próximos seminarios, que será coordinado de acuerdo al calendario ya definido. Los invitamos enviar sus trabajos o propuestas. Estamos también abiertos a incluir presentadores invitados deotros países que puedan relacionarse con el área temática de cada seminario.

FOREWORD

ChileGlobal Seminars UK started in 2013 as an attempt to assemble research about Chile being done in the United Kingdom, which is one of the first destinations for Chileans studying abroad using BecasChile Scholarships. After the launch of this idea in June 2013, a multi-disciplinary group of people joined the organising committee. We started in London, but we quickly realised that there were people interested in this network from different parts of the UK—not only Chilean students but also Chilean researchers, professionals living in the UK and other researchers interested in Chile. This is also the reason why we decided to invest almost half of our funding to cover travel expenses for both presenters and attendants to participate in our seminars, as a way to be as inclusive as possible within the United Kingdom.

By holding the seminars in English, we have been able to open discussion topics to everyone. This openness is one of the main aspects of our organization, which is for everyone interested in collaboration, either as an organizer or a presenter. However, we are also very interested in disseminating what is being done in the UK in relation to Chile to even broader audiences, which is why we started as part of the ChileGlobal network. We are interested in connecting research to Chile's reality in order to help and influence existing and new public policies that can contribute to a sustainable development of the country.

The seminars we have had in London have covered diverse topics and have triggered interesting debates, especially concerning the state of the art of each one of them in Chile. Innovative ideas have been at the centre of these debates, which is why we have decided to compile this book with the content of each seminar. In the index of this book, you will find the list of seminars which represent what is really happening in the UK regarding Chile at the moment, as they have been chosen from the proposals received. As the Encuentros ChileGlobal 2014 Conference is welcoming us in Santiago for the first time, we imagined this book would be a nice way to communicate our experiences with the seminars directly in the Chilean context.

I hope this book can help to bridge the distance between the United Kingdom and Chile and serve as a point of reference for future collaborations in the exciting and diverse research currently being done in relation to Chile.

Bernardita Devilat Loustalot
General Coordinator 2013-2014
ChileGlobal Seminars UK
November 2014

It has been more than a year since the launch of ChileGlobal Seminars UK, which invited everyone to participate in this project with the aim of promoting and disseminating knowledge related to the development of Chile in the United Kingdom. Thanks to this first endeavour, a wonderful team was established to help the academic interchange between professional Chileans and non-Chileans.

The seminars have been organised to tackle one area of knowledge per session, which makes it possible to call for the professional community who have an interest in that area, such as the professionals related to public policy. It has certainly been rewarding for us when professional networks get to know each other and explain their lines of work. This approach is an important step towards integration in the global professional community and gives further opportunities for research.

We certainly have challenges for next year, such as increasing the audience of the seminars and promoting the access to the knowledge repository that is based on the ChileGlobal website. This platform offers a huge potential to have a look at what other communities are doing as well. Therefore, we hope to integrate and collaborate with these initiatives of our colleagues abroad.

We have already run eight seminars, and we are looking forward to the next one on the topic of public health. It is intended to be similar to its predecessors and to bring top-quality research to practitioners, policy-makers and the interested public. I hope you enjoy this book and the next seminars. Your feedback will be welcomed via the ChileGlobal platform (www.chileglobal.net).

Xaviera González Wegener
General Coordinator 2014-2015
ChileGlobal Seminars UK
November 2014

OPEN CALL FOR PRESENTATIONS

Sending an abstract
We invite all researchers working on Chile-related topics to send their information to chileglobalseminarsuk@gmail.com in one Word or PDF file, in English, containing the following:
- Abstract of the presentation (up to 500 words) with images if necessary
- Area(s) of the study (according to the list below) and contact details of the author
- Time availability in which you can present (or indication when leaving the UK)

The abstracts should highlight how the presentation would be organised and framed, and how the subject is relevant for Chile. Another important aspect is how the presentation proposed could trigger an interesting debate among the participants at the end of the seminar. The official language of the seminars is English. The official communication method of these seminars is the ChileGlobal platform: www.chileglobal.net. Thus, participants and presenters are encouraged to register themselves on that platform and become a participant of the initiative there.

Only abstracts sent a month before each seminar will be considered for that specific date. After that, they might be considered for the following events, as the call will remain open and works are expected to be received constantly in order to organise future seminars. The invitation to participate, either as a presenter or as an organiser, will also remain open.

Travel grants offered!
Travel grants will be offered to pay part of the cost of travelling for those who are based in a UK city different from the one where the seminar is being held. The selection criteria will give priority to the presenters and students of the same topic area as the seminars. The available budget will be split between the successful applications. To apply, please send one .pdf file (up to two pages) containing the following to travel.seminarsuk@gmail.com

1. An expression of interest indicating why it is important to participate in the seminar (up to 400 words, not required for speakers).
2. An approximate calculation of the travel costs.
3. Contact details with area of knowledge or work, and indication of the seminar of interest.

The deadline for sending travel grant applications is one week before each seminar.

Questions and comments:
chileglobalseminarsuk@gmail.com
Follow us on twitter:
@ChileSeminarsUK
Facebook: *https://www.facebook.com/UKChileGlobalSeminars*
Website links:
http://comunidad.chileglobal.net/seminars/londres/
http://www.chileglobal.net/categoria/chileglobal-seminars/

LLAMADO A PRESENTACIONES

Enviar un abstract
Invitamos a todos los investigadores trabajando en temas que tengan relación con Chile a enviar su información a chileglobalseminarsuk@gmail.com en un sólo archivo Word o PDF, en inglés, que contenga lo siguiente:
- Abstract de la presentación (hasta 500 palabras) con imágenes si es necesario.
- Área(s) de estudio (de acuerdo a la programación) y detalles de contacto de el(la) autor(a).
- Disponibilidad de tiempo de el (la) autor(a) para presentar, o indicación de hasta cuándo residirá en el Reino Unido.

Los abstracts deberán poner énfasis en cómo la presentación será organizada y cómo el tema es relevante para Chile. Otro aspecto importante es cómo la presentación propuesta puede iniciar un debate interesante entre los participantes al final del seminario. El lenguaje oficial de los seminarios es el inglés. El método de comunicación oficial es la plataforma de ChileGlobal: www.chileglobal.net. Por esto, invitamos a todos los presentadores y participantes a ser miembros de esta plataforma y convertirse en uno de los participantes de esta iniciativa.

Sólo abstracts recibidos un mes antes de cada seminario serán considerados para esa fecha en específico. Después de eso, podrán ser considerados para eventos futuros, ya que el llamado a presentaciones se mantendrá abierto. La invitación a participar, tanto como presentador como organizador también se mantendrá abierta.

Becas de viaje!
Se ofrecen becas de viaje para costear el pasaje (o parte de él) para aquellos que viven en ciudades distintas a aquella donde será el seminario de interés. El criterio de selección dará prioridad a los presentadores y estudiantes de la misma área del seminario. El presupuesto disponible será dividido entre las postulaciones exitosas. Para postular, es necesario enviar un solo archivo PDF (con un máximo de dos páginas) que contenga la siguiente información a travel.seminarsuk@gmail.com

1. Expresión de interés indicando porqué es importante participar en el seminario (hasta 400 palabras, no requerido para presentadores).
2. Un cálculo aproximado de los costos de viaje.
3. Detalles de contacto, incluyendo área de investigación o trabajo, e indicación del seminario en que está interesado(a).

El plazo para enviar postulaciones a becas de viaje terminará una semana antes de cada seminario.

Preguntas y comentarios:
chileglobalseminarsuk@gmail.com
Síguenos en twitter:
@ChileSeminarsUK
Facebook: *https://www.facebook.com/UKChileGlobalSeminars*
Website links:
http://comunidad.chileglobal.net/seminars/londres/
http://www.chileglobal.net/categoria/chileglobal-seminars/

Picture: Bernardita Devilat

I SEMINAR: URBAN STUDIES AND ENVIRONMENTAL REGULATIONS

8th October 2013

Venue: G04. Wates House. The Bartlett School of Architecture. University College London. 22 Gordon Street, London WC1H 0QB.

Chair: Juan Pablo Astorga

Programme:

- **Pablo Salas – University of Cambridge:**
'Climate Change Mitigation Cost or Investment? A Paradigm Shift'

- **Paola Valencia – University College London:**
'Lessons Learned From the UK Residential Energy Efficiency Policy and How These Can Help Develop the Chilean Approach'

- **Néstor Garza – University of Cambridge:**
'Skyscrapers and the Economy in Santiago: 64 Floors of Globalization Agenda'

- **Francisco Vergara – University College London**
'Democratic Cities: Santiago as the Paradox of a Democratisation Process. 1990-2012'

- **Questions and answers, and final debate about the presentations**

Climate Change Mitigation Cost or Investment? A Paradigm Shift

PABLO SALAS AND JEAN-FRANCOIS MERCURE

Accurate opportunity costs estimation is an essential requirement for making successful environmental policies. In a scenario of global economic recession, where budgets are prone to austerity readjustment, any cost overestimation may lead to dangerous budget cuts, jeopardising the effectiveness of the underlying policies. Unfortunately, traditional economic models seem to persistently overestimate the opportunity costs of climate change mitigation measures, associating policies supporting low carbon energy technologies with large economic costs. As a result of these analyses, renewable subsidies and carbon taxes are often seen as economic losses, and therefore policies limiting low carbon technology support are suggested as an alternative. One of the most recent examples comes from Spain, where the energy sector has been strongly affected by the last economic crisis, and the government is proposing a new levy in off-grid electricity generation (which means, for instance, taxing solar panels for households). This is a clear example of how environmental policy, such as subsidies for renewable energy, can be considered too costly, and consequently be overturned in favour of austerity measures.

In the case of developing countries, such as Chile, expenditure in environmental policies is not typically seen as investment but as cost, and therefore, detriment for economic growth. Regarding climate change mitigation policies, it is common to find in economic literature terms such as "mitigation costs" (instead of "mitigation investment"), which show an ex ante assumption that emission abatement policies are costly for the economy, and cannot produce a positive net economic impact. This type of prejudgments are rooted in the traditional economic modelling characterisation of environmental policies, which are typically described using oversimplification of the feedbacks between investment, technology diffusion, employment and economic growth.

Using a disaggregated macroeconometric model of the global economy * , the economic impact of a set of climate change mitigation policies are analysed in this paper, under the scenario of

a 90% reduction of global carbon emissions by 2050 (in comparison with 1990). Based on a dynamic bottom-up representation of the power sector (instead of using traditional optimal equilibrium theory), positive economic effects associated to the decarbonisation of the global economy are found, in contrast with most of the economic projections existing in the literature.

** The economic model is E3MG, a disaggregated macroeconometric model of the global economy (1). It is used together with FTT: Power, a bottom-up model of the global power sector based on market competition, induced technological change and natural resource use and depletion (2).*

References

(1) *Barker, T., Anger, A., Chewpreecha, U. & Pollitt, H. A new economics approach to modelling policies to achieve global 2020 targets for climate stabilisation. Int. Rev. Appl. Econ. 26, 205–221 (2012).*

(2) *Mercure, J.-F. FTT:Power: A global model of the power sector with induced technological change and natural resource depletion. Energy Policy 48, 799–811 (2012).*

Lessons Learned from the UK Residential Energy Efficiency Policy and How these Can Help Develop the Chilean Approach

PAOLA VALENCIA

This study analyses the residential energy efficiency (EE) policy of the UK and Chile, which were introduced several years apart. It attempts to identify possible contributions from the UK experience to the Chilean process. Initially we discuss the history of the UK and the Chilean building and energy institutional framework, policy and the building regulations regarding energy efficiency. The next step was to develop a comparative analysis of their policies and the first plan implemented in each country.

The analysis results show that although the UK historic process of the institutional framework, as well as its policy implementation has been complex, the policy structure is clearer than the Chilean one. The latter has some measures but it has lacks a clear policy to organise those measures as well as programs. In addition, the Chilean residential energy efficiency policy lack of incentives for middle class and also for energy suppliers to implement energy efficiency measures in residential buildings, to contribute with the fulfilment of the national targets. On the other hand, initiatives related to implementing renewable energy in residential buildings, are not mentioned in the Chilean EE plan, although there are some programs of solar thermal energy already implemented.

Finally, a new programme is proposed and evaluated, to commit energy suppliers to implement an economical instrument to encourage the installation of energy efficiency measures in middle-class homes. This programme is specifically focused on implementing solar thermal energy for hot water in residential buildings. This could have a positive impact in the gas consumption reduction, since 78% of gas is imported and the current Chilean energy problem concerns dependence or security, and the programme could also collaborate to achieve the national energy reduction target.

Note: This is part of a dissertation submitted for the fulfilment of the Degree of Master of Science Built Environment: Environmental Design and Engineering. The Bartlett School of Graduate Studies, University College London

Democratic Cities: Santiago as the Paradox of a Democratisation Process. 1990-2012

FRANCISCO VERGARA

In 1990 Chile started a process of social transformation known as Democratic Transition, from Pinochet's dictatorship to a democratic government. With this transformations the expectations on Chilean cities' future, particularly the public spaces, were high among scholars and specialists. At the beginnings of the 90s, the political discourse of the Concertation of Parties for Democracy (Political coalition that leaded this process) was related to social justice, equity, opportunities and democratic social construction. Therefore, assuming that the city is the physical manifestation of the society, it is interesting interpret in which manner the political transformation of the nation triggered spatial transformations, and what is the meaning of these transformations. In other words, what is the democratisation history that the city has recorded in the last 22 years?

The scenario of democratisation in Chile offers several inputs to explore the idea of democratic city, reviewing how the citizens interpret the right to the city and how this interpretation could be addressed to diverse approaches towards the construction of democratic spaces; and to discuss how the production of the city is being developed in Latin America.

Acknowledging the value of democracy as a force of social transformation, and connecting the city production with this ideology, arises a series of questions: What are the components that define a democratic space? Is it possible to design a democratic space in a Latin American Context? As response to these concerns, this paper has been developed to tackle them starting on the abstract construction of the idea of democratic city, to gradually move towards a study case as the "Plaza de la ciudadanía" which permit us to understand how the democratic city as theoretical construction can be interpreted in the built reality. The paradox and the contradiction are present in the production of the democratic Santiago, and the interpretation of this paradox would demonstrate which type of democracy was installed on Chile.

Keywords: Democratisation, Urban Design, Santiago, Plaza de la Ciudadanía, Right to the city, Contested Space.

Summary

This first thematic seminar was in October 2013 and addressed the topics of urban planning and energy regulations. This seminar was chaired by Juan Pablo Astorga and had an audience of about 30 people.

Pablo Salas explained the benefits associated with the de-carbonisation of the Chilean energy sector, not only in environmental terms, but also in relation to the Chilean economy that relies on importing fossil fuels. Paola Valencia compared the energy efficiency policy at the residential level in Chile and the United Kingdom. Néstor Garza presented urban-economic theories explaining the incentives to build skyscrapers, using the Costanera Centre building in Santiago as a case study. Francisco Vergara analysed the concept of democratic cities, using Santiago as a case study.

The presenters suggested the following points with regard to their presentations and the final debate: creating more and better information channels to help the decision-making process regarding who designs the public policies and to help improve social participation; increasing the role of the public sector in the solution of energy problems; and improving the role of the City of Santiago as a democratic space.

Resumen

Este primer seminario temático fue en Octubre de 2013 y abordó las áreas de Urbanismo y Regulaciones Energéticas. Este seminario fue presidido por Juan Pablo Astorga y tuvo una audiencia de alrededor de 30 personas.

Pablo Salas explicó los beneficios asociados a la decarbonización del sector energético chileno, no sólo en términos medioambientales, sino también en relación a la dependencia de la economía chilena al importar combustibles fósiles. Paola Valencia comparó la política de eficiencia energética a nivel residencial en Chile y el Reino Unido. Néstor Garza presentó teorías urbano-económicas que explican los incentivos para construir rascacielos, usando el edificio Costanera Center en Santiago como caso de estudio. Francisco Vergara analizó el concepto de ciudades democráticas, usando Santiago como caso de estudio.

Los presentadores sugirieron los siguientes puntos respecto de sus presentaciones y el debate final: crear más y mejor canales de información, para ayudar en la toma de decisiones de quienes se encuentran diseñando políticas públicas, y también para mejorar la participación social; aumentar el rol del sector privado en la solución de problemas energéticos; y mejorar el rol de la ciudad de Santiago como un espacio democrático.

Notes from the final debate

BERNARDITA DEVILAT

Several comments and questions followed the presentations. One was directed to all of the presenters: What are the one or two things that you would recommend for Chile, bearing in mind that these recommendations would be available in the ChileGlobal network for that purpose? Paola Valencia recommended involving the private sector in the designing of environmental regulations, but not when defining the policies as that should be the role of governments. She also recommended trying to implement social programs for the middle class as they do not have enough funding to implement some measures. Pablo Salas answered that the country is doing well in the area of energy, although we have a big challenge ahead. For the future, he recommended embracing a more global way of thinking instead of focusing only on local issues. The evolution of the energy landscape should be defined by more than only economic considerations. Néstor Garza indicated that Santiago represents a laboratory for other similar cities in the region to learn from. Finally, Francisco Vergara responded that the city has been excluded from the process of democratisation. In 20 years a sense of stability has been created, but the city should be seen as part of that democratisation.

People attending the seminar were also responsive. One of them commented that in Chile the economic powers are highly concentrated and retail is highly controlled, thus it could be interesting to relate that economic power with the idea of building these skyscrapers. It is a sign of a non-democratic process to have the tallest building in the city.

Another participant referred to Pablo Salas's presentation: In the case of the riots and marches against the Patagonia Hidroaysén power station, what is the role of the experts in raising consciousness about the current issues? He replied that, as educators, we have a role not only for ordinary people but also for those that make decisions about the country. 'We need to create more open spaces (not necessarily physical) to connect the people from academia with those who make the public policies', he said. In that regard, Francisco Vergara thought that the role is to inform both sides—

politicians and also social actors—because we need discussion based on information and data. 'We should provide all of them with arguments for the debate. We should find a way to make our research understandable for all, which is quite a challenge', he said.

In relation to Garza's presentation, an attendant mentioned the case of Panama in comparison to Santiago, and asked what would happen to skyscraper construction in the future if more regulations were set on place. Néstor replied that both cases are different. In Panama, the construction has been on empty plots of land. The new high-rises are located on land reclaimed from the sea. In Santiago, it is now impossible to find a big enough plot of land in a good location to build something like Torre Costanera. 'It will be difficult to have the same conditions again, but everything will depend on how much money a risk-developer will be willing to invest in the future', he said.

Picture: Felipe Lanuza

II SEMINAR: DISASTERS, EMERGENCIES AND RECONSTRUCTION

ChileGlobal

14th November 2013

Venue: Room 1.01. Wates House. The Bartlett School of Architecture. University College London. 22 Gordon Street, London WC1H 0QB.

Chair: Bernardita Devilat

Programme:

- **Vicente Sandoval – University College London:**
'Community vs. State in Post-disaster Context: Uneven Outcomes on Environmental Justice and Resilience in Chaitén'

- **Juan Sebastián Lama– London School of Economics:**
'Redistributing Responsibilities. A Comparative Analysis on Public Participation Methods After the 2010's Earthquake and Tsunami'

- **Ignacia Ossul – Techo UK:**
'Earthquakes: Immediate or Permanent Crisis? The Case of TECHO in Slums'

- **Elizabeth Wagemann – University of Cambridge:**
'Transition to What? From Shelter to House After the 2010's Earthquake in Chile'

- **Questions and answers, and final debate about the presentations**

Community vs. State in Post-disaster Context: Uneven Outcomes on Environmental Justice and Resilience in Chaitén

VICENTE SANDOVAL, CLAUDIA GONZÁLEZ AND CRISTIAN ALBORNOZ

In May 2008, the remote city of Chaitén was evacuated due to the risk of a volcano eruption. Few days later, severe floods drove to the destruction of the almost entire city. In the months following the disaster, the Government developed projects which failed into relocate the city to a safer location as well as strategies to support the affected population aimed to improve community resilience.

Contradictory institutional policies as well as unforeseen effects of implemented bond schemes have resulted in a highly segregated and environmentally unjust city where public policies' outputs are unevenly distributed. Thus, this paper addresses how some related processes of increasing resilience might negatively impact environmental justice, hence exploring a potential inverse relationship between resilience and justice.

Five years on, nearly half of the population have returned to Chaitén despite the refusal of the authorities and the city apparently has returned to life. While northern Chaitén concentrates most of the population and investment, 160 families living in the southern Chaitén bear the lack of potable water and other basic services, and are more vulnerable to future disaster impacts. Split in two due to both geography and policies, Chaitén faces now two realities.

Keywords: Chaitén, community resilience, environmental justice, post-disaster policies, vulnerability

Transition to What? From Shelter to House After the 2010's Earthquake in Chile

ELIZABETH WAGEMANN

This paper focuses on transitional shelters built after the 2010 earthquake in Chile and how families have modified them in order to meet their needs during the process of recovery.

The transitional housing solution used in Chile after disasters is called 'mediagua', which is an 18 square meters timber shack built in two days by a group of four people. Long term solutions given by the government usually take place two or more years after transitional shelters are built, and therefore, families remain in these shacks during that time. The 'mediagua' is a fast shelter solution, although usually does not fulfil families' needs that live there during this extended lapse of time. Therefore, users start to modify these shelters with or without support from the government and other institutions, resulting in time and money spent in a house that is intended to be temporary. Although similar transitional shelters have been extensively used by the humanitarian sector in different parts of the world, they have been also criticised because they duplicate efforts and resources, and in some cases they have hindered the achievement of the permanent solution. New approaches have appeared in recent years, such as incremental systems that go from the emergency phase to the permanent solution. Nevertheless, due to the complexity of the housing problem, including land tenure issues, only few successful examples can be found.

Fieldwork was conducted in 2012 in Maule and Bío-Bío regions in order to analyse the requirements of families living in these transitional shelters since the 2010 earthquake. Changes made to the houses were studied through qualitative analysis with the aim of identifying similar patterns in the way they are modified. Most adaptations made by users are related to climatic conditions and cultural aspects. Initial results from this analysis will be presented with final thoughts about how a transitional house may be designed to include future changes and to become (or be part of) permanent housing.

Summary/ Resumen

The second seminar was in November 2013 on the topic of disasters, emergencies and reconstruction. It was presided by Bernardita Devilat. The audience actively participated in the discussion that followed the presentations of Vicente Sandoval, Juan Sebastián Lama, Ignacia Ossul and Elizabeth Wagemann. The main issues raised in the debate are related to the challenges of learning from past experiences, the implementation of disaster reduction strategies, promoting resilience in communities, and better ways to deal with emergencies through new institutions.

El segundo seminario fue en Noviembre de 2013 sobre desastres, emergencia y reconstrucción. Fue presidido por Bernardita Devilat y congregó más de 40 personas, quienes participaron activamente en la discusión que siguió a las presentaciones de Vicente Sandoval, Juan Sebastián Lama, Ignacia Ossul y Elizabeth Wagemann. Los principales temas que surgieron en el debate están relacionados con los desafíos de aprender de experiencias pasadas, la implementación de estrategias de reducción de desastres, promover la resiliencia en las comunidades, y mejores formas de enfrentar emergencias a través de una nueva institucionalidad.

Notes from the presentations and the final debate

RODRIGO CAIMANQUE AND ELIZABETH WAGEMANN

In latest years, Chile has been seen internationally as an example of good practice for facing disasters, specifically about the quality of the building codes and how they have been implemented in a rigorous way. Nevertheless, researchers working on disasters, emergency and reconstruction in Chile know that there are still space for improving the processes, the coordination and the approaches. After the presentations, an audience of around 40 people participated actively in a discussion focused on: how to learn from past experiences; how to implement disaster risk reduction strategies and promote communities' resilience; and future approaches for facing emergencies through new institutions.

The cases of Chaitén (after the volcano eruption) and Juan Fernandez (after the tsunami) were taken as examples from which to learn. With the former, learning from the contradictions and difficulties of the post-disaster plan, and with the latter, from the success of the participatory design approach. The second part of the seminar was focused on the process of transitional shelter construction and its effects in both the short and long term.

During his presentation, Vicente Sandoval pointed out that early top-down decisions taken by the government in Chaitén had an impact in the way families affected responded to later indications, and this will possibly affect future responses. The creation of a special committee from the central government to face the post-disaster process triggered tensions with regional and local authority decision-making, for instance, through the relocation of communities in a new settlement. Contradictions emerged in the way the recovery was conducted, such as the reoccupation of the affected areas, which created a new conflict in terms of the state's U-turn concerning the occupation of the land. This has caused the population to have a lack of confidence and credibility in the state—eroded trust— meaning possible problems in future decisions in the case of new risks, such as evacuation.

The case of Juan Fernández was presented by Juan Sebastián Lama as a successful case of participatory design, where the designers and the community worked closely together on the project from the beginning of the process. Through a comparative case study, it was stated that from similar starting points (initial proposals from the state and experts to address the disaster), different processes were performed in relation with communities, with different levels of success. The comments from the audience were that being a small community and also an island defined a more cohesive group in this case, and therefore created an easier environment for a public participation scheme. The case of Talca was shown as a different experience where the possibilities of participation were diminished, possibly due to its population size among other reasons.

In the second part of the presentations, Ignacia Ossul presented the work carried out by the NGO 'TECHO' in the construction of 20,000 transitional shelters after the 2010 earthquake and tsunami in Chile. The challenge was met by a massive voluntary movement in the south of the country. The mapping of shelter locations and clear accountability were relevant during the process in order to provide data for definitive housing in a more transparent process. However, there is controversy in terms of the role of the state and NGOs in the process of reconstruction, and how 'transitional' or 'permanent' the new shelters are. Finally, Elizabeth Wagemann critically addressed this topic through an accurate analysis of the transitional shelters' features, providing both advantages and disadvantages of the construction and typology. The process of shelter adaptation done by local communities towards new definitive housing is evidence that there is a gap between the positions of the government, NGOs and planners about the use of shelters, while from the community perspective the solutions seem clearer.

After the presentations, the panel discussed that when the design and planning for reconstruction is only defined by experts without input from the population affected and without approaching communities, the definition of the problem is biased in the way it is addressed, and

there is a lack of comprehensiveness. When this happens, it is difficult for the communities to get involved because they do not have the possibility to define their problems and the main concepts that will drive the reconstruction.

Another topic for discussion was the need to improve public policy to face disasters in a country with different risks, such as volcano eruptions, earthquakes, tsunamis and floods. What are the roles of the state, the third sector and civil society when an emergency affects the country? The identification of the root causes of vulnerability, the definition of plans to risk reduction, and participatory plans for reconstruction should be included in political agendas. In general, government approaches have a clear top-down focus for emergencies; however, it is necessary to open up the debate and analysis to a more bottom-up understanding of disasters, as the Juan Fernández case illustrated.

In academia, there is currently an interest to do research on these topics, and it was mentioned in the debate that two centres were created at the Pontificia Universidad Católica de Chile, CIGIDEN (Centro de Investigación para la Gestión Integrada de Desastres Naturales) and Universidad de Chile, CIVDES (Centro de Investigación en Vulnerabilidades y Desastres Socionaturales). Nevertheless, in general, there is still a focus on emergency and post-disaster action rather than prevention, though there have been some improvements in these aspects.

Finally, the need for new institutional arrangements in order to address risk and disasters as well as prevention was discussed. Some ideas were discussed, such as the creation of the Ministry of Emergency, Disaster Reduction and Reconstruction or specific departments dealing with these topics in each ministry, leading towards a more multi-sectorial cooperation and coordination. The understanding of the complete cycle would be essential to keep track of the process and lessons learned throughout the years. In that case, an inter-ministerial organisation with a more holistic vision would be an approach to explore.

Picture: Bernardita D

III SEMINAR: BIOTECHNOLOGY AND MEDICAL SCIENCES

20th February 2014

Venue: Medical Sciences G46 H O Schild Pharmacology LT. University College London. Gower Street, London WC1E 6BT

Chairs: Stephanie Braun and Mauricio Zamorano

Programme:

- **Jorge Soza-Ried – Imperial College London:**
'Using Cell Fusion to Understand Reprogramming'

- **Jessica Ocampos – University of Cambridge:**
'Investigation of Preservation Method Developed in Chile for Vitrification of Human Spermatozoa with Emphasis on Reproductive Medicine'

- **Deborah Navarro – Imperial College London:**
'Nutrition-Chronic Related Diseases in Chile: The Link Between Obesity and Cancer'

- **Questions and answers, and final debate about the presentations**

Using Cell Fusion to Understand Reprogramming

JORGE SOZA-RIED

Cell fusion-mediated reprogramming of somatic cells toward pluripotency is rapid and efficient yet poorly understood. In particular, the importance of cell cycle and DNA synthesis for epigenetic reprogramming has until rather recently, remained largely unexplored. Here we used centrifugal elutriation to enrich mouse ES cells at progressive stages of the cell cycle, and showed that S/G2-phase enriched ES cells are more efficient at reprogramming somatic cells in heterokaryons and hybrids assays. This reprogramming success was associated with an ability to induce precocious nucleotide incorporation by somatic nuclei within newly formed heterokaryons. BrdU pulse-labeling experiments revealed that virtually all successfully reprogrammed somatic nuclei, identified on the basis of Oct4 re-expression, had undergone DNA synthesis within 24 hours of fusion with ESCs. This was essential for reprogramming as drugs that inhibited DNA synthesis blocked pluripotent conversion. Collectively, these data show that the reprogramming capacity of ES cells varies according to cell cycle stage and that early DNA synthesis is a critical event in the epigenetic reprogramming of somatic cells in experimental ESC-heterokaryons.

Investigation of Preservation Method Developed in Chile for Vitrification of Human Spermatozoa with Emphasis on Reproductive Medicine

JESSICA OCAMPOS

Many cell based applications have arisen in recent years because of the increase of the aging population and the consequent high demand on healthcare treatments. Three main cell based applications have gained great importance: regenerative medicine (particularly stem cell applications), biotherapeuticproduction(recombinant proteins, products from cells), and cell biobanking. Those application fields require reliable preservation systems that guarantee high cell viability after preservation, with predictable recovery of normal cell functionality. However, to date those conditions are not often accomplished and hence the requirement for improvements or changes in preservation protocols. The only cell protectant technology that provides reliable long term cell stabilisation is cryopreservation, using temperatures below -80°C to minimise degradation [1]. This process is traditionally accomplished using high concentrations of permeant cryoprotectant agents (CPA). This technology presents several limitations that have stimulated the search for improvements in biopreservation. The most commonly used cryoprotectant, DMSO, has been associated with different negative side effects. In the case of regenerative medicine, the high concentrations of this protectant can adversely affect transplant patients. Therefore it is necessary to remove it before transplant to the patient, which implies a costly process [2].

Note:
Collaborative work between Department of Chemical Engineering and Biotechnology, University of Cambridge, Pembroke Street, Cambridge CB2 3RA, United Kingdom; and Department of Chemical Engineering and Biotechnology and Universidad de la Frontera (UFRO), BIOREN, CEBIOR, Temuco, Chile.

References

[1] J. P. Acker, "The use of intracellular protectants in cell biopreservation," in Advances in Biopreservation, New York, Taylor & FrancisGroup, 2007, pp. 299-320.

[2] S. S. Buchanan, M. A. Menze, S. C. Hand, D. W. Pyatt y J. F. Carpenter, "Cryopreservation of Human Hempatopoietic Stem and Progenitor Cells Loaded with Trehalose: Transient Permeabilization via the Adenosine Triphosphate-Dependent P2Z Receptor Channel", Cell Preservation Technology; 3, 2005, pp. 212-222, 2005.

Nutrition-Chronic Related Diseases in Chile: the Link Between Obesity and Cancer

DEBORAH NAVARRO

Chile has undergone a demographic and nutritional transition. Its population, once mostly young and undernourished, is now older and overweight. This phenomenon is linked with the high prevalence of nutrition-related chronic diseases that mark the country. Forty years ago, the most common cause of death was infection-related disease.
According to the National Health Survey (2004), only an average of 20% of Chilean primary school student consumes fruits and about 30% consume vegetables in the last seven days. On the other hand, an average of 38% of these children consumed fizzy drinks.

The 2010 follow-up National Health Survey showed that the population's current eating patterns of the Chilean population are having an impact on health. The results of this survey showed that 39% of Chileans are overweight and 25% are obese. Among chronic diseases, cancer is the most lethal and the main cause of mortality and disability in most developed and developing countries. In the case of Chile, cancer is among the three most common causes of death and hospitalisation.

A number of dietary, nutritional and physical activity factors are associated with cancer incidence and mortality. According to the World Cancer Research Fund (http://www.wcrf.org/), between 30% and 40% of cancer cases in adults are preventable. Body fatness is a transversal risk factor for most cancer types (like breast, colorectal, pancreas, endometrium, ovary, and gallbladder), equally affecting men and women.

Chile shows the highest incidence and mortality of gallbladder cancer among women in the world. Gallbladder cancer is associated with body fatness along with genetic and other factors. The link between gallbladder cancer and obesity is extremely important in a country like Chile, where more than 50% of the population exhibits obesity or overweightness. This rate is even greater when we refer only to women (45% showing overweightness and 30% showing obesity).

Colorectal cancer is also highly prevalent in Chile. According to the Chilean Ministry of Health's data from 2011, colorectal cancer is the only cancer type in Chile whose incidence increases with patients' age. As Chile's population is drastically ageing, this is an important factor for policymakers to consider. It is crucial that Chilean stakeholders introduce effective interventions to reduce obesity population-wide. On the same note, stakeholders, academics and health professionals must be made aware of the link between cancer and obesity.

Summary

The third seminar was in February 2014; it had an audience of 25 people and was presided by Stephanie Braun and Mauricio Zamorano. The presenters were able to explain in a simplified way—for the audience in general—highly complex and specific issues, which is key since the seminar was meant to be for people from different areas of expertise. At the seminar, the presenters focused on specific topics: Jorge Soza on cellular reprogramming; Jessica Ocampos on cell cryopreservation; and Deborah Navarro on the relationship between obesity and cancer. One important aspect that came out was the lack of access to information and medical databases in Chile (which are a key input to the research) and the need for these to be systematic, representative and credible. Both the public and the presenters themselves emphasised the importance of seminars to disseminate what science and medical science researchers are doing in the United Kingdom for Chile. This is especially important as each seminar is on a specific subject area and discussions can be in greater depth. They also emphasised the importance of knowing who is leading this research and working to generate possible future collaborations, both academic and practical.

Resumen

El tercer seminario fue en Febrero de 2014, contó con una audiencia de 25 personas y fue presidido por Steffi Braun y Mauricio Zamorano. Los presentadores lograron explicar de manera simplificada para la audiencia en general- temas altamente complejos y específicos, lo cual es clave, puesto que ésta estuvo integrada por personas de diversas áreas del conocimiento. Se discutieron preguntas específicas relativas a cada presentador: Jorge Soza sobre reprogramación celular; Jessica Ocampos sobre criopreservación celular; y Deborah Navarro sobre la relación entre obesidad y cáncer. Un aspecto importante que salió en ellas fue la falta en el acceso a la información y a bases de datos médicas en Chile, que son un insumo clave para la investigación, la necesidad de que éstas sean sistemáticas, representativas y fidedignas. Tanto el público como los propios presentadores destacaron la importancia de los seminarios para difundir lo que se está estudiando y haciendo en ciencias duras y médicas en el Reino Unido para el país. Esto es importante sobre todo porque al ser cada seminario en un área temática específica, los debates pueden también llegar a un mayor nivel de profundidad en los contenidos. Asimismo, destacaron la importancia de conocer a quienes lideran estas investigaciones y trabajos para así generar posibles colaboraciones futuras, tanto académicas como prácticas.

Notes from the final debate

STEPHANIE BRAUN AND MAURICIO ZAMORANO

(Q: question / A: answer)

Using cell fusion to understand reprogramming

Q: What is the difference between reprogramming with Yamanaka factors and fusion?
Jorge Soza (A): Both methods can be used to reprogram somatic cells towards a pluripotent-like state. Induced pluripotent stem cells have great potential to be used for regenerative therapy and drug discovery purposes. However, due to its low efficiency and delay in identifying successfully reprogrammed cells, it is not the best route to define the early events of reprogramming. Cell fusion, albeit with no clinical applications, is a simple and more efficient approach that allows examination of the early events that occur in the somatic nucleus during successful reprogramming.

Nutrition-chronic related diseases in Chile: the link between obesity and cancer

Q: What is the measurement for child obesity used in the figures?
Deborah Navarro (A): The measurement is the BMI (body mass index), but the thresholds for defining underweight, overweight and obesity in adults (aged 18 years and above) and children (aged 2–18 years) are different because the growth rate and shape of children's bodies change between birth and adulthood.

Q: Where I can find information on the number of cancer patients in Chile?
Deborah (A): Sometimes primary cancer is not diagnosed correctly, which will make it impossible to find that information and there is no access to medical records. You can consult the Cancer Registry, but it doesn't include all cancer cases.

Final message from the speakers

Jorge Soza:
It is important to have meetings, such as this seminar, to get to know each other. I think we should be more connected with Chilean students and professionals around the world to share ideas and develop projects. In order to promote research in Chile, it is necessary to build successful networks between Chilean researchers in Chile and abroad, and provide a direct route for students' exchanges and collaborative projects. In this respect,

we need researchers that stay abroad and this is as important as our need for professionals to go back or develop their careers in Chile. However, to succeed in this it is essential to create an environment of willingness to collaborate. It is necessary to share our results and views of future research without fear of creating competition. The Chilean government or public entities and universities should provide easy access to information. At the moment, it is extremely difficult to find out what kind of research is being done in Chile.

Jessica Ocampos:

It is important to get to know each other to overlap research areas and create new ideas and knowledge. The government should apply a long-term strategy to improve the high technology level in the country through highly qualified professionals and motivating scientists from different areas to work in Chile.

Deborah Navarro:

In Chile it is necessary to promote the operation of top-class research institutes. Institutions should consider assessing the background and experience of professionals and not only their professional titles. We should broaden our minds. Chilean researchers living in other countries should have the opportunity to show their work in Chile and make it known.

General comment:

A general concern of Chilean researchers doing PhDs or postdoctoral studies in the UK who are supported by the Becas Chile funding is that they are obliged to return to Chile, where their fields are not that open or developed. It is indeed an opportunity, but when someone is actually starting a career it is also a step backwards in terms of the scientific productivity, opportunities and diversity of research. In many situations, a researcher in science can do so much more 'real' collaboration or contributions to Chile by developing a career abroad, forming an active network that can bring students from Chile for internships, organising meetings inviting Chilean professionals, and so on, instead of going back to a non-existent niche in Chile.

Picture: Bernardita Devilat

IV SEMINAR: MUSIC

6th March 2014

Venue: Embassy of Chile. 37-41 Old Queen Street SW1H 9JA London, United Kingdom

Chair: Marcos Stuardo

Programme:

- **Welcome by the Consul, Sebastián Lorenzini, and the chair of the session, Marcos Stuardo**

- **Katia Chornik– University of Manchester:**
'Musical Commemorations of the Fortieth Anniversary of Pinochet's Coup'

- **Ernesto Calderón – Director of Transatlantic Ensamble:**
'The Folk Music in Chile'

- **Questions and answers, and final debate about the presentations**

- **Musical performance of Transatlantic Ensamble**

Musical Commemorations of the Fortieth Anniversary of Pinochet's Coup

DR. KATIA CHORNIK

An unprecedented number and variety of commemorative events have taken place this year around the fortieth anniversary of the onset of Augusto Pinochet's seventeen-year dictatorship, coinciding with major changes in the ways in which Chilean society remembers this period and its legacy, particularly in relation to abuses to human rights. Using recent personal interviews and footage, and drawing on revival theory, this paper examines two events happening in Santiago: the carnivalesque act of a 70-piece troupe of musicians and dancers called 'Los diablos rojos de Víctor Jara' ('The Red Devils of Víctor Jara') at a multitudinous street rally, and the re-founding and performance of a choir of political prisoners (originally formed in 1976 in Tres Álamos detention centre) at a memorial in Villa Grimaldi, one of Pinochet's most notorious torture chambers.

The Folk Music in Chile

ERNESTO CALDERÓN

In today's modern Chile, many things have changed since the return of democracy (1990). Music is having a huge role in shaping new society, and the youth are getting more access than ever to develop their skills and show their work. Government-driven initiatives like the Youth and Children's Orchestras of Chile Foundation (2001), the creation of the Arts & Culture Council (2003), and the Fund for the Promotion of National Music (2004) are showing results, and together with many independent projects, are giving to Chile the most lively music scene it has ever had.

Together with this, since 2006, Chilean musicians have been participating in different 'Ethno' music projects, in countries such as Sweden, Scotland, Slovenia, Belgium and Germany, giving as a result a growing interest these kind of projects, and the beginning of new Ethno-inspired initiatives in Chile. In 2012, a new orchestra, the Transatlantic Chilean Folk Ensemble, was created with musicians from different regions of Chile and abroad, playing a newly composed Chilean-based repertoire, and with a line-up and live performance that very much resembles an Ethno orchestra.

The project expanded quickly, having more than 100 participants in less than a year, and in 2013 it was launched in Europe, with many members who were active participants of Ethno camps. As a result it has formed a global community of folk musicians interested in Chilean and Latin American music, combining it with their own traditions and musical background, encouraging the creation of new compositions and sonorities, and creating a constant exchange of experiences and knowledge that benefits everyone involved.

Summary

MARCOS STUARDO

This session featured two presentations followed by a short musical act by the Transatlantic Chilean Folk Ensemble. The first presentation, led by Dr. Katia Chornik and entitled 'Musical Celebrations of the Fortieth Anniversary of Pinochet's Coup' dealt with Chornik's reflections and findings regarding the musical work of 'Los Diablos Rojos de Victor Jara' (Victor Jara's Red Devils) and a choir formed by former political prisoners of 'Villa Grimaldi', one of the numerous camps created under Pinochet's regime. 'Los Diablos Rojos' propose a re-reading of Victor Jara's songs and a translation of his music into a new aesthetic, mainly based on 'diabladas' and 'bailes chinos', traditional music from the northern part of Chile.

In his presentation, Ernesto Calderón reflected on his musical career and how it has led him to the creation of the 'Transatlantic Chilean Folk Ensemble', a musical group based both in Chile and Europe, which aims to disseminate Chilean-inspired folk music, performed both by Chilean and foreign musicians. Ernesto has shown how music has the power to unite people of different cultures, languages and traditions through artistic reflection. One of the ensemble's key principles is to perform without scores. This manner of working has been highly valued by the performers, especially by those trained in the classical or academic tradition who have been faced with a purely aural method of learning music.

This seminar has taught us that music is not an innocent act alienated from the rest of society. The musical practices of the groups studied by Dr. Chornik are full of political content, and are carried out by people who share clear political and moral ideals. In the same way, the Transatlantic Chilean Folk Ensemble constitutes a vivid example of how the Chilean culture can be publicised around the world and, therefore, it is necessary to give more support to musicians, composers and cultural managers so they can perform their work abroad. Chilean artists and academics have the important mission of being ambassadors of their land in remote corners of the planet.

This seminar was organised in close collaboration with the Embassy of Chile for the UK. Additionally, it has had the special collaboration of Dana Brablec Sklenar, who is a member of the organizing committee of the ChileGlobal Seminars UK.

Resumen

Gran entusiasmo y profunda reflexión fueron las principales características que los dos oradores transmitieron a los asistentes el día del evento, el cual se realizó en las dependencias de la Embajada de Chile en Londres. La ponencia de la Dra. Katia Chornik versó sobre las "Celebraciones Musicales a los 40 Años del Golpe Militar en Chile", mostrando como ejemplo el trabajo de "Los Diablos Rojos de Víctor Jara", quienes proponen una re-lectura del trabajo artístico del cantautor, haciéndolo dialogar con otras estéticas musicales como las "diabladas" y "bailes chinos", típicos de las celebraciones religiosas del norte de Chile y del coro "Voces de Rebeldía", conformado por ex prisioneros politicos de Villa Grimaldi.

Por otro lado, el compositor popular y acordeonista Ernesto Calderón, reflexionó acerca de su trayectoria musical y como ésta le ha llevado a la creación del "Ensamble Transatlántico de Folk Chileno", agrupación con base en Chile y en Europa, que tiene como fin la difusión de música popular de inspiración chilena, interpretada tanto por músicos chilenos como extranjeros. Ernesto ha demostrado cómo la música puede unir a los pueblos de diferentes culturas, lenguas y tradiciones por medio de la reflexión artística. La peculiar forma de trabajar de esta agrupación ha sido muy valorada por los intérpretes de "tradición clásica o académica", quienes se han tenido que enfrentar a una nueva forma de aprender las piezas musicales, esto es, sin partituras, sólo de manera auditiva. Este seminario nos ha enseñado que la música no es un acto inocente de creación artística, autodefinido y sin relación con el medio. La práctica musical de las agrupaciones estudiadas por la Dra. Chornik están cargadas de contenido político comprometido, y son llevadas a cabo por personas que comparten los ideales políticos y morales de las izquierdas. Asimismo, el Ensamble Transatlántico de Folk Chileno es una clara muestra de que la música es una gran forma de dar a conocer la cultura chilena alrededor del mundo y, por consiguiente, se hace necesario dar más apoyo a los músicos, compositores y gestores culturales que ejercen sus labores en el extranjero, cumpliendo la valiosa misión de ser embajadores de su tierra en alejados rincones del planeta.

Este seminario fue organizado en estrecha colaboración con la Embajada de Chile en el Reino Unido. Además, se ha contado con la colaboración especial de Dana Brablec Sklenar, parte del comité organizador de los ChileGlobal Seminars UK.

Music Performance of Transatlantic Ensamble

Picture: Bernardita Devilat

ChileGlobal

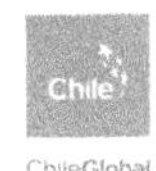

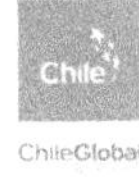

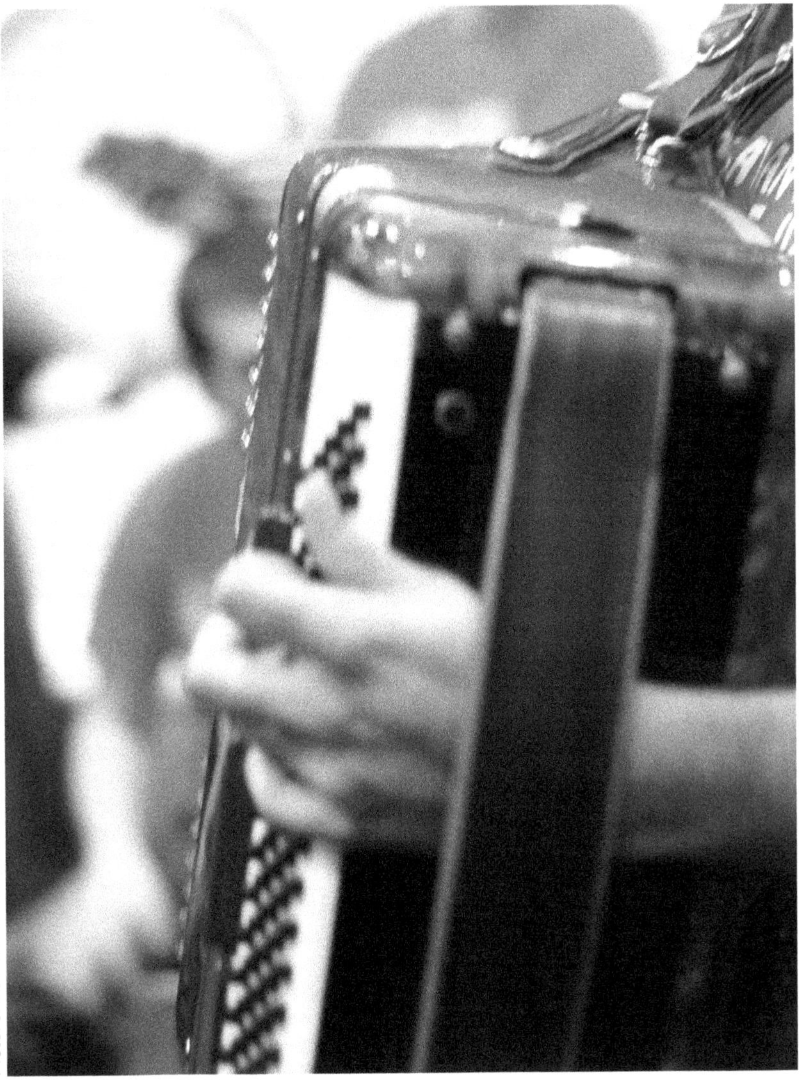

Picture: Bernardita Devilat

Picture: Bernardita Devilat

V SEMINAR: EDUCATION

22nd May 2014

Venue: Room 822 (level 8), Institute of Education (IOE), 20 Bedford Way, London WC1H 0AL

Chair: María Jesús Inostroza

Programme:

- **Marigen Narea – B. London School of Economics and Political Science:** 'Early Child Care and Child Cognitive and Socio-Emotional Development: Evidence from Chile'

- **Natalia Torres C. – University of Sheffield:** 'The Concept of Early Childhood Education in Chile: Reproduction and Refusal of Policies by Key Actors'

- **Ximena Galdames C. – Institute of Education, University of London:** 'Problematising Chilean Early Childhood Education by Exploring How Normative Discourses of 'the Child' are Performatively (Re)produced in the Classroom'

Questions and answers

- **Álvaro González T. – Institute of Education, University of London:** 'A Balancing Act. The Principles and Practical Orientations of External Support for Educational Improvement in Chilean Schools'

- **Juan de Dios Oyarzún M. – Institute of Education, University of London:** 'Tensions Between Schools and Individuals: An Applied Study at La Legua Neighbourhood'

Questions and answers, and final debate about the presentations

The Concept of Early Childhood Education in Chile: Reproduction and Refusal of Policies by Key Actors

NATALIA TORRES

Since the return of democracy in Chile, educational reforms have been in the centre of social interventions, and the two core reform concepts used in this period were quality and equality. Nevertheless, even though there was an interest on using education as a platform for social change with the state playing an active role in its promotion, policies designed during the dictatorship and heavily influenced by market laws remained in force, producing tensions and contradictions in the educational system.

In terms of research, a lot has been done regarding the analysis of these tensions, but a more comprehensive understanding of the concepts of quality and equality has been less approached by researchers as well as by policy makers. Specifically, during the last 10 years, Early Childhood Education (ECE) has been at the centre of educational public policy development in Chile, positioning it as a major concern amongst policy makers and researchers, but although education policies have explicit purposes that seek the integral development of children and the fulfilment of learning outcomes, impact research has shown that these are not being achieved and several factors have been investigated as possible causes, not focusing on a more critical analysis of the way that policies are being designed in the first place, and if these policies actually promote the outcomes that are being sought.

For this reason, my research focuses on the assumptions behind the design of ECE policies in Chile, looking at the process from a critical perspective, analysing why is ECE taking such an important role in the educational agenda and what are the concepts that policy makers are using when thinking about ECE policies? What are the ideas, beliefs and concepts present in head teachers, teachers, parents and children about ECE and the policies implemented? And ultimately, how these different assumptions and definitions relate to each other (if they do) and how they influence the implementation of ECE policies, and their outcomes?

My approach is explicitly critical, and thus, my goal is to analyse these concepts in terms of power relations, that is, who is defining

quality and equality and under what assumptions? How these concepts relate to the ones that educators, children and teachers have? How these concepts also relate to larger social structures, reinforcing and/or refusing the actual status of education in Chile and its contradictions? Using a critical ethnography methodology and resting on the ideas of a critical research approach, including collaborative and participatory methods in order to take in the voices of all different actors involved in ECE, as active players in the development of ECE policies in Chile.

In this presentation, I aim to explain these key factors and also engaging Chilean education researchers in the discussion of them, and how we as researchers should approach the analysis of public policies in education, taking into account these tensions and contradictions present in their design and implementation.

Problematising Chilean Early Childhood Education by Exploring How Normative Discourses of 'the Child' are Performatively (re)Produced in the Classroom

XIMENA GALDAMES

The Chilean field of early childhood education (ECE) suffers from an apolitical and predominantly motherly stance (Galdames, 2010) which impedes working towards social just practices within education, because it frames its practitioners, children and their families within oppressing and unjust conditions (Galdames, 2011). Looking at the Chilean case of how discourses of 'the child' are shaped or emphasised through global neo-colonial and/or neoliberal forces is relevant for Chile and other countries in development which have to follow global tendencies of universalising ECE and care provision to compensate for social inequities and promote social justice (Dahlberg and Moss, 2005). The shapes that ECE and care have taken, impact on children's lives and subjectivities, attempting to 'make' them subjects for this rationale. By exploring how these discourses shape children, female educators and researchers, but also how they are resisted and transformed; offers alternatives for reconceiving pedagogical and curricular practices in everyday interaction in the ECE classroom.

Thus, I attempt to disrupt 'the compulsory adult/child dualism' and acknowledge the concept of child 'as political' (Cannella et al, 2000, p. 219). The foundations of Chilean ECE curriculum, which –informed by westernised, Eurocentric, white, sexist and postcolonial notions- have established regimes of truth about 'the child' and therefore configure the discursive production of particular individuals within ECE contexts (Galdames, 2012). Thus, normalised ideas of 'the child', 'childhood' and 'children' have constituted and regulate(d) the Chilean ECE field (epistemologically and ontologically), and therefore also children's and practitioner's lives (Cannella, 1997): a specific subject ('the child') that has to be (re)produced within ECE classrooms. However, I query that these discourses are not simply reproduced and regulated, but also resisted and transformed within everyday interactions.

I problematise these ideas in my current study which articulates a postmodern approximation to ethnography, autoethnography and play (as a participative research method). Critical nods of the study (in progress) will be shared, the context is: the classroom of a publicly subsidised nursery, situated within a vulnerable

area of a Chilean urban setting. 32 children aged three to four and four practitioners are the participants. I also consider myself within the sample, as I participate as an adult researching woman, former child, student and practitioner; and therefore contributes and (re)creates subjectivities, which may be violent towards the individuals they subjectivise, generating unjust conditions and situations within the classroom.

I will present extracts from my field notes and auto ethnographic diary and play, to illustrate how my argument about the naturalisation about 'the child' in ECE, violently impact in the constitution of individuals (children and adults) in the ECE classroom, and therefore contributes and (re)creates subjectivities, which may be violent towards the subjectivised individuals, generating unjust conditions and situations within the classroom. I will also question if the discursive positions available in the classroom are resisted and/or transformed by us, therefore creating the possibility to modify the normative interpellation, and thus discourses of 'the child'.

A Balancing Act. The Principles and Practical Orientations of External Support for Educational Improvement in Chilean Schools

ALVARO GONZÁLEZ

With the intention of improving the equity conditions and quality of education, and levelling the playing field for disadvantaged schools, the Preferential School Subsidy Law (SEP) allocates, since 2008, extra funding to municipal- and private-subsidised schools catering for deprived children in exchange for developing an improvement plan that will achieve standardised targets in terms of education outcomes (Ahumada, 2010; Contreras & Corbalán, 2010; Raczynski, Muñoz, Weinstein, & Pascual, 2013). Additionally, the recent implementation of a law that creates a National System of Quality Assurance of (SNAC) in Chile altered the role of the Ministry of Education (MINEDUC) and Council of Education (CNED), and created two new institutions: the Superintendence and Quality Agency. These structural and governance changes, added to Ministry initiatives interventions, configure a particular policy framework for promoting educational improvement in Chilean schools (Acuña, Assael, Contreras, & Peralta, 2014; Astudillo & Imbarack, 2013)

Building on two qualitative research experiences I conducted with Chilean municipal primary schools, in this paper I aim to discuss the influence of this policy framework on schools that receive external support for improvement. The first is a single case-study of primary school working with a university-based provider of education technical (ATE) conducted in 2010, which focused on the influence of the relationship between school staff and external agents in the process of improvement. The second is a multiple-case study of three programmes of external support implemented in two urban municipalities in Chile, which is still in progress, and its focus is on the influence of the policy framework in the practice of schools and external support programmes. Both studies consisted of in depth-interviews, questionnaires and documentary analysis (Bassey, 1999) with relevant actors from schools, external support programmes, municipal and ministry officials; and the analysis strategy consisted of a case description (Yin, 2003).

I will approach the policy framework from two perspectives. Firstly, I will present the tension between different drivers for improvement presented in policy documents, and will address the origin of this tension by analysing the principles underpinning the policy framework, which are rooted on effective school improvement literature (Chapman, 2005; Fullan, 1992; Hargreaves, 2001; Hopkins, 2001; Reezigt & Creemers, 2005). I will concentrate on three issues here: the role of the school on the improvement process, the combination of top-down and bottom-up approaches, and the role of external support to trigger educational improvement. Secondly, I will present some vignettes to describe how this policy framework translates into practice from the perspective of the activities external support programmes implement in and with schools. Here, I will argue that the practice of supporting school improvement is played largely on two competing practical orientations: updating and installing competences, versus building and supporting internal capacity in schools.

Finally, I will argue that these principles and practical orientations are relevant to understand the current state of educational improvement policy in Chile, and to promote a sustainable practice of improvement in disadvantaged schools.

Tensions Between Schools and Individuals: An Applied Study at La Legua Village

JUAN DE DIOS OYARZÚN

This study stands La Legua neighbourhood, in Santiago, and seeks to answer the question: What kind of cultural dynamics explain the school dropout? This will be developed through a qualitative methodology, from interviews with young people and school directives in 2011. From the characterisations of young students and schools, the results sought to detect the relationships and tensions between individuals and institutions, as one of the causes for understanding the break and school dropout.

So, the study is framed in terms of the sociology of culture, considering the tension between institutions and individuals, from the sociological theory of individuation. In this tension, the narrative plays a mediating role between the two levels of analysis: on one hand, realise the cultural processes occurring at the institutional level of society, and on the other, accounts for the processes of individuation between individuals.

Thus, this research is introduced into the sociological and educational theme of the dropout phenomenon. The premise is based on this phenomenon, although multi -causal, is rooted in an institutional dynamic that fails to cover the entire population on which has to respond as training and education service. Institutions not only educate, claim, form (include) individuals, but otherwise exclude, form an individual by marginalisation, by a failed relationship.

Therefore, the study addressed the processes of individuation within youth who interrupted their schooling process, taking as axis approach the narrative of individuals, and moreover the narrative of educational institutions, according to the student profile to forge, the educational project and its disciplinary, academic and training mechanisms created as part of a formal education process. The research is aimed to check disagreements and contradictions between the stories founded, as analytical and real indicators of tension, which in one way or another led to the failure of the school experience of individuals.

Education is a constitutional right for all Chilean citizens; school dropout is a breakdown of such rights and a symptom of a possible failure of the Chilean education system. Similarly, no access to certain goods, services and public rights by a significant proportion of our society, is definitely an issue of high relevance to political, ethical and sociological levels, thus defying the social sciences to question about this phenomenon, examine its causes and consequences, and thus illuminate the problem, delivering valid information for the proposal of solutions and appropriate responses to the matter.

This research is about La Legua neighbourhood, located in the district of San Joaquín, Santiago city, known in the media as a place of violence and drug trafficking, which have generated numerous police interventions. Therefore, there were studied young people and schools located within the neighbourhood and surrounding area. This geographical definition was taken to illustrate the social and educational reality in a relevant place of society, as there are different types of social marginalisation, which show the weaknesses of our development model, as well as the limitations of the public and private offering in various subjects of public policies, rights and benefits.

To show the school as a major player in the reality of school dropout, to the detriment of visions that point out responsibilities mainly in individual, family and micro-social aspects of the young students' lives, suggests being important information to assess this institutional break and exclusion. Beyond each particular case, this study sought to indicate certain structural weaknesses of the educational system in our society, and to learn more about the life and motivations of young students in La Legua as voices made visible in a context that is repeated in many other social spaces of this country.

Summary

MARÍA JESÚS INOSTROZA

The seminar approached two main topics, namely early childhood education (ECE) and the impact of policy on schools and students. The first part of this seminar dealt with the question of the concept of 'quality' in ECE. Marigen Narea discussed the effects of early care on children's cognitive and socio-emotional development. Her research showed there was an association between a positive impact on cognitive development and a negative impact on socio-emotional development for those children attending day care (versus maternal care) between 24 and 36 months old. However, this would vary depending on socio-economic status, with those children from the second quintile of income benefiting the most from centre-based care. Narea's main argument challenges the expanding centre-based care coverage and argues for rigorous evaluation of the quality of early childhood education and care services.

The second speaker was Natalia Torres, who focused on the theoretical background and design of her research project. Torres's study dealt with the beliefs and reasons behind the implementation of ECE policy, as well as the teachers, parents and children's views on its implementation. According to her, researchers should approach the analysis of public policies in education by taking into account these tensions and contradictions present in their design and implementation.

In the final presentation on ECE, Ximena Galdames challenges the concept of 'the child' in the Chilean ECE curriculum, and presented it as political one. This concept configures the discursive production of particular individuals within ECE contexts; therefore, constituting and regulating children's and practitioner's lives. Galdames argued that the naturalisation of 'the child' in ECE violently impactsthe constitution of individuals (children and adults) in the classroom, and therefore does not contribute to the diversity of subjectivities within the classroom.

The second part of the seminar started with Alvaro Torres's presentation on the influence of the policy framework for educational improvement in schools that receive external support. Torres presented the evidence from his study on Chilean schools. He argued that there were tensions between what is allowed in and expected from schools that have access to external support. Similarly, schools struggle with updating and installing competences, and building and supporting internal capacity in schools.

Finally, Juan de Dios Oyarzún referred to the dropout phenomenon in a study carried out in la Legua village in Santiago. Oyarzún argued that tensions and disagreements between individuals and schools as institutions impact on the schooling process of young people.

Questions and discussion

Early Childhood Education (ECE)
There is a question on the government insisting on increasing the coverage of ECE, despite the policy aspects of the history. Marigen explained that coverage is the easiest way to do it, and it is the first thing to do. She exemplified with the tough response she had received from policy makers when she was presenting results that did not agree completely with the idea that all children benefit from attending ECE.

There is a clarification of terms, such as centre-based care, as well as the distinction between education and care. The latter is a very broad definition that includes any formal type of care in a group setting. More than 80% of children attend centres and there are many differences between them. Care is an important element in centres, particularly for younger babies.

Reflection on the reasons why children from lower income families stay with their mothers instead going to ECE shows a link to low-paidwork. Marigen mentioned that mothers prefer to stay with their children rather than spend time and money on transport. Similarly, it is mentioned that in centres the group setting is very stressful and the level of noise is also very high.

The discussion developed interesting questions on the data collection process. For example, Natalia referred to the incorporation of the voice of children in her research. She explained that she stands from the new sociology of childhood; therefore by using a participatory methodology, she wanted to incorporate the voice of children or adults talking about their children as key actors of ECE. Similarly, Ximena described how she dealt with herself as a research-participant during data collection and analysis in the research. She said it was really challenging, going back and forth, and mentioned that she used a diary. Ximena pointed out that it was very difficult to differentiate because her actions contributed to and were affected by the data.

The underlying reasons for reconceptualising quality and equity in Chilean policies were mentioned. Natalia explained that from the analysis on educational reforms and documentation it was possible to see some evidence of change from the days of the dictatorship. However, the new policies still maintain old policies. There has been a reconceptualisation of the concepts, but they are still very broad and global.

Regarding the discourses on normativity, the notion of flexible identities of a post-structuralist perspective was mentioned. Ximena explained that during data analysis she realised that these discourses were much more structured in her thoughts, and that it was difficult to keep track of the difference. She exemplified with the discourse between two participants in which she could find pedagogical, gender, violence and romantic elements.

Policy, schools and individuals

The external support teams for school improvement come from different backgrounds; they are not necessarily teachers, and they have different experience and different agendas. They may be experts in a specific field, but not necessarily teachers. Most of them have an educational degree.

Reflecting on the variables involved in these implementation processes, Alvaro explained that the internal realities varied between schools. People from outside are seen as having a comparative advantage over them. He also mentioned that from the internal perspective they are very selective about who goes there and who does not. Teachers feel that they have to compete.

Juan de Dios explained that both schools in his study were failing their students. They were similar in regard to socio-economic status, with students rotating between them. With the Catholic school, students felt a real rejection, but in the other schools there was a kind of disaffection. He identified a very rigid itinerary towards the labour market in the Catholic school. This school clearly knew how to be part of the job market. In contrast, he said, the other schools seemed to be extremely open, and they did not seem to have a structure. This lack of structure impacted on a lack of expectation from the students.

Relevance of this seminar

After the student demonstrations in 2011, quality has been identified as a key concept for education. However, it is unclear what it entails. This seminar challenged concepts such as quality and equity that seem to be defined broadly by policy makers. The different presentations tackled issues regarding deeper changes in education, which are supported by evidence from the Chilean context. The relevance of this seminar is that it allows us to contribute to policymaking and critically question the current measures for improving the school experience of Chilean children and young people.

Picture: Bernardita Devilat

VI SEMINAR:
APPLIED TECHNOLOGIES IN MEDICAL SCIENCES

5th June 2014.

Venue: Pearson Lecture Theatre (North East Entrance). University College London. Gower Street, London, WC1E 6BT, UK

Chairs: Jessica Ocampos and Stefan Pszczolkowski.

Programme:

- **Keynote Speaker: Dr. Cristina Navarrete, National Head of H&I Services, Director of British Bone Marrow Registry (BBMR), Scientific/Deputy Director of NHS Cord Blood Bank:**
'Cellular Therapy and Its Application in Bio Banking'

- **Dr. Andrés Herane – Institute of Psychiatry, King's College London:**
'Cortisol Secretion Patterns In Hair: The Biomarker Of The Future In Mood Disorders? A Systematic Review'

- **Sebastián Aguayo – University College London:**
'Use of Advanced Microscopy for Characterization of Oral Bacteria on Dental Implants'

- **Deborah Navarro – Imperial College London:**
Open Debate: 'Facts and Myths about Thimerosal: The Case of Chile'

- **Questions and answers, and final debate about the presentations**

Cellular Therapy and its Application in Biobanking

DR. CRISTINA NAVARRETE

Picture: Bernardita Devilat

Cortisol Secretion Patterns in Hair: The Biomarker of the Future in Mood Disorders? A Systematic Review

DR. ANDRÉS HERANE

The role of stress on health and its contribution to the development of mood disorders is highly controversial. Most studies looking at chronic stress and its effects on mood disorders have used either inappropriate scales or biological specimens which do not accurately reflect chronicity. The use of hair is proposed as a novel specimen, where cortisol levels can be obtained and averaged out over relatively long periods of time, therefore representing chronic levels of this hormone. Obtaining these chronic levels will allow better understanding of the role of stress in stress-related conditions and disorders. This review makes an attempt at synthesising all the published studies on hair cortisol concentration related to stress and some psychiatric disorders; particularly in mood disorders. It describes and summarises their findings in the aim of providing a clear picture of the current state of this line of research. This review uncovers a potential for certain disorders -like major depressive disorder- to show hypercortisolemia, while others reveal a potential hypocortisolemia (posttraumatic stress disorder and general anxiety disorder). Hair cortisol concentration shows promise as a specimen to differentiate between different subtypes of affective disorders, and may help further unravel the biological links between stress and related psychiatric conditions, helping diagnosis, prognosis and treatment. Future directions in this area are described. Importantly, this review proposes a new biomarker: the combination of hair and saliva measures of cortisol as a possible complete and specific pattern for each subtype of affective disorders.

Keywords: Hair cortisol mood disorders

Andres Herane Vives, Dr., Institute of Psychiatry/ King's college London, United Kingdom (Presenting);
Valeria De angel, Ms, Universidad de Chile, trastornos del animo, Chile;
Andrew Papadopoulos, Dr., Institute of Psychiatry/ King's college London, United Kingdom;
Danilo Arnone, Dr., Institute of Psychiatry/ King's college London, Psychological Medicine, United Kingdom;
Allan Young, Prof., Institute of Psychiatry/ King's college London, Psychological Medicine, United Kingdom
Tony Cleare, Prof., Institute of Psychiatry/ King's college London, Psychological Medicine, United Kingdom

Use of Advanced Microscopy for Characterization of Oral Bacteria on Dental Implants

SEBASTIÁN AGUAYO

Despite current efforts, tooth loss remains a problem affecting adults around the world as a result of socioeconomic, health and lifestyle factors. In Chile, according to the Health Ministry, approximately 80% of adults aged 35-44 have at least one tooth absent. Although there are many conventional treatments available, the rehabilitation with titanium-based dental implants is the preferred therapeutic option for replacing single or multiple missing teeth.

Many surface modifications have been developed to enhance the biological and mechanical properties of implants, mostly by increasing surface roughness; however, this also favours bacterial colonization and infection. It is widely accepted that one of the main reasons for implant failure is the formation of a complex biofilm on its surface. Therefore, it is important to understand the interaction that occurs between different bacterial species and titanium surfaces to work on different ways to counteract this process.

Many techniques have been used to study adhesion and interaction of oral bacteria to surfaces; however, most of them employ large number of bacterial cells and thus fail to provide significant information on the principal forces behind cell adhesion. The introduction of the atomic force microscope (AFM) in microbiology has opened exciting new approaches for studying the nano-mechanic behaviour of bacterial cells. The AFM provides a reliable method for probing adhesion forces between cells and surfaces at the cellular and sub-cellular level.

The focused ion beam (FIB/SEM) is currently being used for the study of biological samples. The ability to mill and remove specific areas of a sample for depth and subsurface imaging opens new possibilities for application in dental implant research.

The presentation will cover:

- Causes and consequences of tooth loss
- Use of titanium dental implants for rehabilitation: advantages and disadvantages
- Use of AFM and SEM/FIB to evaluate biofilm colonization of dental implants
- Relevance for Chile: future work and technology

This presentation can open an interesting debate on how to integrate science and innovation to Public Health Care dentistry in Chile. Developing local technologies with direct implication in implant dentistry could provide our country with cost-efficient treatments for our population.

Open Debate
Facts and Myths about Thimerosal: The Case of Chile

DEBORAH NAVARRO

The aim of this lecture is to heighten awareness of the importance of vaccine development in our daily lives. Thimerosal is an organic compound of mercury that works as antiseptic and antifungal in vaccinations against, among other diseases, diphtheria, tetanus and influenza. It is also used in allergy patch testing. In the body, it is metabolised or degraded to ethylmercury (half-life of 18 days). Thimerosal was first used in vaccinations in the 30s.

In 1998, British gastroenterologist Andrew Wakefield published a report on a small number of patients who, following immunisation against measles, mumps and rubella, had developed autistic regression and suffered diarrhoea.

Fuelled by the power of the Internet, the controversy soon reached the US. Here, parents of autistic children and a parallel network of parents' groups opposed to compulsory immunisation, expressed concern over the purported phenomenon.

This apparent discovery was later named as "The most damaging medical hoax of the last 100 years" in prestigious medical journal.

Chilean Members of Parliament, together with a Chilean NGO, starting a debate and to push a removal of all vaccines with thimerosal in the Chilean public health system. They didn't succeed.

If the Chilean government had agreed to discontinue using vaccines containing thimerosal, this could have increased the risk of local outbreaks of long-eradicated infectious diseases, including measles, pertussis and polio. This, in turn, would have triggered a rise in child mortality.

This debate will apply an evidence-based medicine approach to the case of thimerosal usage in Chile, examining how policymakers failed to address this issue based on current and reliable scientific evidence.

Summary

JESSICA OCAMPOS AND STEFAN PSZCZOLKOWSKI

During her presentation, Dr. Navarrete mentioned the advances in cell therapy and stem cell therapy, which are currently in clinical trials, in addition to new research on obtaining adipose tissue stem cells. Regarding this, the ethical issues associated with the consent of the patient and other ways of obtaining cells as altruistic donations were discussed. During the round of questions, the audience asked about the state of the art in Chile with respect to these techniques. Dr. Navarrete responded that there is indeed knowledge and know-how in Chile. In fact, one of the best scientific publications on the topic is from Chile (by Dr. Alejandro Erices), in addition to work being carried out at the Clinical Hospital of the Pontifical University Catholic of Chile and at the Calvo Mackenna Hospital.

After this presentation, Dr. Andrés Herane showed a review about how the measurement of levels of cortisol in hair can help distinguish whether a patient suffers from some psychiatric or mood disorders. It is important to highlight that this would refer patients with simple mood disorders to psychological therapies, in order to avoid the prescription of psychotropic drugs to those who do not require them.

Sebastián Aguayo's work corresponds to a study about the use of atomic force microscopy in the study of bacterial adhesion on titanium dental implants. This will allow the creation of implants that are more resistant to bacterial colonization.

Finally, Deborah Navarro spoke about the myths and truths of thimerosal, a mercury-derived compound that acts as a preservative in vaccines, and how its use affected the population in the case of Chile. Of particular relevance is the fact how this controversy has affected the perception of some parents and political authorities regarding the safety of vaccines in general, and the potential health problems that would occur if children are not vaccinated anymore in the country.

These key points were stressed in the panel of questions and answers with the four speakers. First, the contribution and impact of this area of knowledge in the reality of Chile. Second, the importance

of maintaining a relationship with the national contingency, which includes collaborations between Chilean and foreign centres. Third, the contribution that Chilean postgraduates students abroad can make to maintain this collaboration. Fourth, the role of students, researchers and academics as experts in their areas of research to give opinions and help in important decisions at a nationwide level which have an impact on health. Finally, the importance of discussion between experts, society and authorities.

Importance of this seminar

Throughout the union of technology and medicine, great strides in cell therapy, imaging and diagnostic systems for disease management have been made, in addition to the use of software and information technologies for this purpose. On the other hand, these kind of seminars allow people in the area of technology— which does not necessarily have a 'hard' background in health or biology—to be part of multidisciplinary groups and to contribute based on their own knowledge.

Conclusion

As researchers, it is imperative to share our knowledge with the community, generate interest, clarify concepts and keep them informed, particularly about the impacts of any decision involving technical, technological and scientific issues. Even though we are outside Chile, our responsibility is to keep ourselves informed and expose our observations, always on the basis of scientific evidence. Our responsibility is even greater because we are in a really privileged position.

Resumen

Durante su presentación, la doctora Navarrete mencionó los avances en terapia celular, en terapia con células madres, que actualmente están en clinical trials, además de las nuevas investigaciones en la obtención de células madres de tejido adiposo. Respecto de este tema se discutió sobre los temas éticos asociados al consentimiento del paciente y respecto a otras maneras de obtención de células como donaciones altruistas. Durante la ronda de preguntas, se consultó sobre estado del arte en Chile respecto de estas técnicas, a lo cual la Dra. Navarrete respondió que de hecho hay conocimiento y know-how en Chile. De hecho que una de las mejores publicaciones científicas es chilena, del Dr. Alejandro Erices, además de trabajos que se están realizando en el Hospital Clínico de la Pontificia Universidad Católica de Chile y en el Hospital Calvo Mackenna.

A su vez, el Dr. Andrés Herane presentó una revisión acerca de cómo la medición de niveles de cortisol en el pelo pueden ayudar a diferenciar si un paciente padece trastornos del ánimo o algún desorden psiquiátrico. Es importante destacar que esto permitiría derivar pacientes con simples trastornos del ánimo a terapias alternativas (psicológicas) y así evitar la prescripción de psicotrópicos a quienes no lo requieren.

El trabajo de Sebastián Aguayo corresponde a un estudio acerca del uso de microscopía de fuerza atómica para el estudio de la adhesión bacterial en implantes dentales de titanio. Esto permitirá crear implantes que sean más resistentes a la colonización bacterial.

Finalmente, Deborah Navarro expuso acerca de los mitos y verdades del Timerosal, un compuesto derivado del mercurio y que actúa como preservante de vacunas, y de cómo su uso afectó a la población en el caso de Chile. De particular relevancia es el hecho de cómo esta controversia ha afectado la percepción de algunos padres y autoridades políticas respecto de la seguridad de las vacunas en general y el potencial problema sanitario que resultaría de dejar de vacunar a los niños del país.

En el panel de preguntas y respuestas con los cuatro expositores se destacó:

- La contribución e impacto de esta área del conocimiento en la realidad de Chile.
- La importancia de mantener una relación con la contingencia nacional, lo cual incluye las colaboraciones entre los centros chilenos y extranjeros.
- El aporte que los estudiantes chilenos de postgrados en el extranjero pueden hacer para mantener esta colaboración.
- El rol de los estudiantes, investigadores y académicos como expertos en sus áreas de investigación para dar opinión y ayudar en decisiones importantes a nivel país, que impacten en salud.
- La importancia del sentido crítico y de la discusión entre expertos y la sociedad y las autoridades.

Importancia de este seminario

Gracias a la unión de tecnología y medicina se han logrado grandes avances en terapia celular, imagenología, diagnóstico y sistemas de manejo de enfermedades, además del uso de software y tecnologías de información para tal propósito. Por otra parte, este tipo de seminarios permite que personas del área tecnológica, que no tienen necesariamente un background 'duro' en salud y/o en biología puedan formar parte de grupos multidisciplinarios y contribuir desde sus conocimientos.

Conclusión

Como investigadores, es un deber compartir nuestros conocimientos con la comunidad, generar interés, aclarar y mantenerlos informados. En especial los impactos de cualquier decisión que involucre temas técnicos, tecnológicos y científicos. Si bien nos encontramos fuera de Chile, nuestra responsabilidad es mantenernos al tanto y exponer nuestras observaciones, siempre sobre la base de evidencias científicas claras. Incluso nuestra responsabilidad es mayor, pues nos encontramos en una posición realmente privilegiada.

Picture: Pabla Cornejo

VII SEMINAR: ENGLISH AS A FOREIGN LANGUAGE IN CHILE

15th October 2014

Venue: Elvin Hall, Institute of Education, University of London. 20 Bedford Way, London WC1H 0AL

Chairs: Álvaro González and Ximena Poblete

Programme:

- **María Jesús Inostroza – University of Sheffield:**
'Developing Listening and Speaking Skills when Teaching English to Young Learner in Chilean Large Classes'

- **Pía Tabalí – University of Warwick:**
'Practical Ways of Incorporating Learner Autonomy into the Chilean Primary School English Lessons'

- **Loreto Aliaga-Salas – University of Leeds:**
'Exploring English Language Teaching in Pre-Service TELF Education in Chile'

- **Lucas Ríos Santana – King's College London:**
'Queering EFL Chile: A Dialogue between Queer Theory and Chilean EFL Teachers' Perceptions of and Practices Around Sexual Identity Issues in the Classroom'

- **Elizabeth Torrico-Avila – University of Southampton:**
'English Language Teaching and Economic Development in Chile'

- **Keynote speaker: Dr. Richard Smith – Associate Professor at the Centre of Applied Linguistics, University of Warwick**

- **Questions and answers, and final debate about the presentations**

Developing Listening and Speaking Skills when Teaching English to Young Learner in Chilean Large Classes

MARÍA JESÚS INOSTROZA

In the last few decades, the number of countries that have incorporated EFL as part of their compulsory Primary Education curriculum has steadily increased. Similarly, a wide range of literature has been published for teaching English to young learners (TEYL), understood as 5 to 11 year-old.

The teaching environment in many countries, however, is often characterised by large classes, limited resources, and unqualified teachers. Many publications have focused on large classes, mainly to identify their difficulties. This negative perspective, however, has provided little discussion about how TEYL is impacted.

Chile has developed a curriculum of EFL teaching for primary and secondary education, which is compulsory from Quinto año básico (around 10 years old); in 2012, however, the Ministry of Education (MINEDUC) launched a suggested curriculum from Primero to Cuarto Año básico (from 6 to 9 years old). Similarly, the English Opens Doors programme managed by the MINEDUC supports teachers and students of state-run and subsidised schools in the development of their language skills. Even though Chile is implementing different ways to improve the language skills of their students, little research has been done in this field.

Considering this context, this research project has been carried out in Chile, with the purpose of identifying the applicability of well-known activities to develop listening and speaking skills when TEYL in large classes, particularly in state-run or subsidised schools in Santiago. Currently, the data collected is being analysed.

Practical Ways of Incorporating Learner Autonomy into the Chilean Primary School English Lessons

PÍA TABALI

In this globalised world, English has been established as the lingua franca in which to communicate (Harmer, 2000; Brown, 2007). Therefore, the teaching and learning of this language has become a major issue around the globe. During the last decade, there has been a sudden tendency to start teaching English at earlier stages. Moreover, many countries have decided to include within their school policies the teaching of English as a main subject from an early age (Yuliana, 2003). This seems to follow the demands from governments, syllabus designers and parents (Cameron, 2003). Despite this shift of interest, some scholars (e.g. Rixon 1999a; b; Garton et al., 2011) have agreed on the pronounced need to further research the way children learn.

One way of addressing this issue is to work on more child-centred approaches, looking for ways to foster children's autonomy. The benefits of enhancing children's autonomy in the language classroom are inevitably relevant regarding the world they live in. Young Learners (YLs) must be prepared for the rapid changes of our society, since their teachers and parents will not be always there to protect them. According to Bergen (1990) autonomous learners who have learned how to learn, would be able to apply that knowledge in any learning situation they may encounter, not only during their school life, but also as lifelong learning. In this sense, the responsibility of teaching children how to learn relies mainly on schools, since they must equip learners with the strategies to be used in and out of the school context (Pinter, 2006).

In relation to the Chilean local context, little has been done in order to address the issue of fostering children's autonomy. In order to delve into this reality, the aim of this presentation will be to introduce how activities that would foster children's autonomy through metacognitive processes, such as planning, monitoring and evaluating, could show young learners' reflection on their own processes of learning English. The data will be based on the results of an intervention carried out in Chile with students from second grade of a primary school. This presentation bring a later debate on different issues in the Chilean education system, such as the appropriateness of teaching English to children in Chile, the methodologies used, our national conception of childhood, listening to children's voices and the importance of developing more research devoted to investigate young learners and their unique way of learning.

Exploring English Language Teaching in Pre-service TELF Education in Chile

LORETO ALIAGA-SALAS

This presentation will focus on the impact of an integrated curriculum in a TEFL (Teaching of English as a Foreign language) programme for trainee teachers in Santiago, Chile. The talk will show the current TEFL curriculum at Universidad Alberto Hurtado, implemented in 2011. The main characteristic of this programme is the integration of contents of "hard" areas i.e. literature, lexical grammar, and culture into the language courses. These no only focus on developing language proficiency, but also knowing about the language. Moreover, the programme sees the integration not only at the language course levels, but also at all the areas involved in the path of a trainee teacher, i.e. linguistics and methodology, practicum, humanities and education.

This curriculum is based on CLIL (Content and Language Integrated Learning), an emphasis on the cognitive academic learning of the language, CALLA (Cognitive Academic Language Learning approach), the text-based and task-based approaches and the lexical approach. The assessment mostly focuses on the task-based approach, for it gives students the opportunity to practice language, using all their language resources instead of just one particular item. As a consequence, students' experiences in the classroom with the language become more meaningful and relevant and their exposure to the target language is higher.

In addition, the presentation will also deal with the issues and challenges of a curriculum change considering all the actors and levels, i.e. department authorities/ coordination, teachers, and trainee teachers. Some of the issues have been the lack of coordination among teachers, a higher time demand for material and test design, as well as meeting students' demands, interests, and needs.

The main challenge still remains to be the inclusion of the hard areas within the task-based approach which are more a context for students to show whether they are able to use rather than know this knowledge. Another important concern at the academics level is

that even though they support the new curriculum at a discourse level, what happens in the classroom may be different to what it is promoted by the decision-makers and coordinators.

All in all, the main objective of this research is to evaluate the effectiveness of this curriculum reflected in the trainee teachers' performance in the classroom, replicating how they learned at university, and consequently, reflected on their school students' learning.

Queering EFL Chile: A Dialogue between Queer Theory and Chilean EFL Teachers' Perceptions of and Practices around Sexual Identity Issues in the Classroom

LUCAS RÍOS SANTANA

Since 1990, inclusive education has been relevant in Chile with the return to democracy so as to offer an education that includes everyone regardless of their differences. For instance, in 1998, the Education International World Congress passed a resolution on the 'Protection of the rights of lesbian and gay education personnel' which focused not only on educational employees themselves, but also on promoting education against prejudices, discrimination and harassment. The Chilean Teachers' Union supported this resolution and together with the Ministry of Education, they have been fighting for inclusion in schools in Chile implementing new policies. Moreover, in 2012 the Chilean government passed a law, known as Ley Zamudio, which penalises arbitrary discrimination, being relevant against discriminatory educational practices. However, poststructuralists and queer theorists critique inclusive practices as they only seek to incorporate those referred to as minorities in education without unearthing discourses that treat those minorities as inferior, and without considering the fact that those groups should not be homogenised, as that would create fixed notions of their identities (for example Youdell, 2006; Allan, 2008; Britzman, 1995). Moreover, recent research in second language acquisition based on poststructuralism (see Block, 2003, 2007; Norton, 2010) understands that our identity is (re)produced by language, thus an important factor that impacts on language learning/teaching is our identity. Specifically about sexual identities, drawing on Queer Theory, some authors (for example Nelson, 2009; Merse 2013, 2014) suggest the use of queer approaches in English language teaching in order to reveal heteronormative discourses enacted in our language and the language being learnt, so as to, for instance, improve language learning. Importantly, these approaches are relevant for teachers of English as a second/foreign language because they can help students develop the types of fluency required to take part in contemporary discourses. Therefore, this study draws upon qualitative data collected in July through email interviews, generating online narratives, from

five different Chilean EFL teachers, who have been working in secondary education in private-subsidised schools in Chile.

Drawing upon Queer Theory, this study creates a dialogue between the data collected from teachers and the different queer approaches. The results indicate that these teachers do not address issues of sexual identity in classes either as part of the contents of them or when tackling homophobia without unveiling the reasons for these discriminatory practices. Also, their perceptions of the issue are in regards to inclusive education therefore limited to only include so-called sexual minorities. Hence, when queering these teachers' practices and perceptions, it can be noticed that their invisibilisation of the issues and their approach could enhance heteronormative discourses and thus reinforce power relations.

Keywords: EFL, Queer Theory, Education in Chile, Queer Education, Queer ELT

English Language Teaching and Economic Development in Chile

ELIZABETH TORRICO-ÁVILA

In 2012, Ricento stated that language policy researchers need to understand how neoliberal economic policies affect the fate of global and local languages (2012:31). According to him, the understanding of how transnationals, corporations, international organisations and policies of states that comply with neoliberal economic model and values influence language practice is limited. Some research has been introduced on the subject and is opening the field for further investigation. For example, Bruthiaux (2002) shows that learning the native mother-tongue in low income countries is more relevant than learning English. Conversely, Brutt-Griffler (2005) disagrees with Bruthiaux and Phillipson's (1991) position stating that people should learn English if it helps to alleviate poverty. Moreover, Pennycook (2004) mentioned that according to his research people with competence in English and some other skill, i.e. a profession or an occupation, succeed in a globalised economy. While Blommaert (2009) reported on successful skilled professionals whose strong foreign accent limited their job opportunities. Therefore, we can conclude that English as a tool for social and economic mobility will depend not only on the economic and political context of its speakers, but also on the speakers' individual skills.

Since 1975, Chile's economy has been based on the neoliberal model of de-regulation and free market. The nation has signed many Free Trade Agreements with many countries, such as The United States of America, (Harvey 2005, 2007). Due to the size and needs of this global economy, Sergio Bitar, former Minister of Education, stated that "... el Inglés es una habilidad clave para pertencer al mundo globalizado" (La Nación, 2003). This statement is the beginning of the EODP which has required the investement of large amount of resources. Still, in 2011, Bitar emphasised the importance of the programme and mentioned that Chileans had to learn English "to sell what [we] are doing, understand and learn from others" (Baker, 2011). In this context, I aim not only to explore the political economic reasons that triggered the introduction of the English Open Doors Programme (henceforth EODP) in Chile in 2003, but also to problematise them.

The methodology to carry out this research is the following: first, the data is elicited from two Chilean newspapers. They are La Tercera and La Nación. Both represent opposing ideologies. Second, the method for coding the data is facilitated by the software called NVIVO. Finally, the analysis is based on Critical Discourse Analysis as this research encompasses the main principles of the CDA approach. They are ideology, power and discourse. The analytical tool for systematising the CDA analysis is argumentation theory (Fairclough and Fairclough, 2012) which reconstructs the argument and makes its fallacies explicit.

Keywords: Neoliberalism, economic development, ELT, EODP, education, discourse.

Summary

ÁLVARO GONZÁLEZ , XIMENA POBLETE AND MARÍA JESÚS INOSTROZA

The seminar approached three main topics. The first referred to English as a foreign language in Chilean Primary Schools. María Jesús Inostroza discussed the perception of teachers about the use of group work during English lessons in Chile. Here, she highlighted the low frequency of this format of work due to problems such as big classes, time limitations and the poor training teachers receive in the use of these strategies. On the same topic, Pía Tabali presented the results of a pilot study about the promotion of students' autonomy in learning English through the use of structured tasks by which children reflect on their learning process and teach themselves among peers.

The second topic discussed in the seminar referred to pre-service training and professional identity of English teachers. Loreto Aliaga discussed the main challenges in the initial training of English teachers in a private university in Santiago, Chile. The curriculum main characteristic is the Integrated English Language course (IEL), which merges the 'traditional' subjects from the linguistics tradition such as grammar and phonetics, with culture. As a result, the IEL course concentrates over 60% of the total hours of the curriculum, and most teacher trainers. Aliaga presented the issues emerged from this curriculum implementation, such as teacher trainers' resistance; conflicting assessment design, proctoring and marking, which have made an impact in trainees' progress along the courses; and the graduate profile current feasibility. The presentation of Lucas del Río discussed Chilean English teachers' perceptions working in secondary education. Based on Queer Theory, Rios created a dialogue between the data collected from teachers and queer inquiry. His reflection was focused on the ways in which subjectivity is reproduced in a second language. The ways in which issues such as equality, inclusion, inclusive pedagogy, rights and acceptance of differences were at the centre of the study.

The third topic argued about the ways in which the political discourse justifies the necessity that Chile must become a bilingual country, imposing English as a second language under the assumption that it is essential in order to participate in the global economy. Elizabeth

Torrico's presentation argued about the relevance of recognising the economic and development discourse that underlie the policies that promote teaching English as a foreign language in Chile.

The seminar was also the centre of the presentation of the Network of Chilean Researchers on English Language Teaching (RICELT). RICELT aims at pointing out the relevance of creating a knowledge community in ELT in Chile. School teachers, university teachers, undergraduate and postgraduate students, and MINEDUC (English Open Doors Programme, EODP) are involved in this network.

Finally, Dr. Richard Smith gave his impressions and comments about the different presentations and highlighted the RICELT initiative as an innovation that is grounded from the professionals who are teaching, which implies an egalitarian approach of sharing information among the different actors involved in teaching English.

The following was discussed in the question panel:

- A reflection about the methodology and the research process used.
- The importance of reviewing whether the curriculum suggested for teaching English is relevant for teachers and students.
- The duration (5 years) of pre-service programmes for English teachers was discussed, as it seems too long in comparison with international programmes.
- The controversy that may imply talking about identity according to queer theory terms was pointed out by the audience.

Relevance of this seminar

Since the beginning of 2000, managing the English language has been positioned as a tool for the economic development of the country, as argued in Elizabeth Torrico's presentation. With this conviction, Chile has invested in programmes and policies to promote English learning. However, despite the investment, the country has been unsuccessful in increasing the number of people who speak English. The relevance of this seminar is that it allows us to critically question why these measures have failed to promote the English language in Chile, from the perspective of the teaching and learning process in the classroom.

Conclusion

Teaching English has been raised as a central topic in the development of the country. This has led to teaching English becoming compulsory from the 5th grade (around 10 years old). This has brought important debates about the pedagogic strategies to teach English in Chilean classrooms and about teaching training to reach the standards. Likewise, promoting this language stresses the need to review the theories and motivations that underlie these policies and how they affect the teaching-learning process. The creation of RICELT shows the relevance of this topic and the necessity for the actors that participate in this process to be part of a research community.

Resumen

El seminario abordó tres grandes temas. El primero se refirió a los métodos de enseánza del inglés en escuelas chilenas. María Jesús Inostroza discutió acerca de la percepción de los docentes sobre el uso de trabajo en grupo en las clases de inglés en Chile. Aquí se destacó la baja frecuencia de este tipo de formato debido a problemáticas como cursos numerosos, limitaciones de tiempo y la baja capacitación de los profesores en el uso de estas estrategias. En esta línea temática, Pía Tabali presentó los resultados de un estudio piloto sobre la promoción de la autonomía de los estudiantes de inglés en Chile a través del uso de tareas estructuradas en las que los niños se enseñan entre pares.

La segunda línea temática abordada en el seminario se relaciona con la formación e identidad profesional de los docentes que enseñan inglés. Loreto Aliaga discutió los principales desafíos de la formación inicial de los profesores de inglés en Chile y cómo se ha enfrentado a través del Curriculum Integrado, donde el 60% de éste se dedica a la rama de lenguage. La presentación de Lucas Ríos abordó las percepciones y prácticas de los profesores de inglés en Chile sobre temáticas queer en la sala de clases. Su reflexión se centró en las maneras en que se (re)preduce la subjetividad en un segundo idioma. De qué manera se abordan temas como igualdad, inclusion, pedagogía inclusiva, derechos y aceptación de las diferencias fueron el centro del estudio.

La tercera línea temática abordada en el seminario se relaciona con la forma como se justifica desde el discurso político la necesidad de que Chile se convierta en un país bilingue, imponiendo el inglés como segunda lengua con el justificativo de que es imprescindible para participar de la economía global. La presentación de Elizabeth Torrico abordó la importancia de reconocer el discurso económico y de desarrollo que subyace a las políticas que promueven la enseñanza del inglés en Chile.

El seminario fue además el centro de la presentación de la Red de Investigadores sobre English Language Teaching (RICELT).

Para finalizar el seminario el Dr. Richard Smith comentó las presentaciones realizadas por los expositores y además destacó la iniciativa de RICELT como una innovación que nace desde los profesionales que enseñan, lo que implica una forma igualitaria de compartir información entre los distintos actores involucrados en la enseñanza del inglés.

En el panel de preguntas se destacó:
- La reflexión sobre la metodología y los procesos de investigación.
- La importancia de revisar si el curriculum que se sugiere para la enseñanza del inglés es relevante para profesores y estudiantes.
- La duración (5 años) de los programas de formación inicial de los profesores de inglés cuestionando si ésta es adecuada, pues parece ser muy extensa comparada con programas internacionales. Frente a esto se planteó que en el caso de Chile la duración del programa parece adecuada, considerando el nivel de entrada de los estudiantes.
- Se cuestionó también qué ha pasado con la política para un país bilingüe como Chile
- La controversia que podría implicar hablar sobre identidad in términos de la teoría queer.

Importancia de este seminario

Desde inicios del 2000, el manejo del idioma inglés se ha posicionado como una como una herramienta para el desarrollo económico del país, como lo argumentaba Elizabeth Torrico en su presentación. Con esa convicción se ha invertido en programas y políticas para promover que la gente aprenda inglés pero, a pesar de los recursos invertidos, no se ha logrado aumentar significativamente el número de personas que hablan inglés en el país. La relevancia del seminario está en que nos permite indagar por qué estas medidas para promover el inglés en Chile no han surtido efecto desde el punto de vista de su enseñanza en escuelas y liceos.

Conclusión

La enseñanza del inglés se ha levantado como un tema central para el desarrollo del país, lo que ha implicado la obligatoriedad de la enseñanza de este idioma desde 5° básico. Esto ha traído importantes cuestionamientos sobre las estrategias pedagógicas para enseñar este idioma en las salas de clases en Chile y la preparación de los docentes para cumplir con los estándares. Asimismo, la promoción de esta lengua releva la necesidad de revisar las teorías y motivaciones que subyacen a estas políticas y de qué manera esto afecta el proceso de enseñanza-aprendizaje del inglés. La creación de RICELT da cuenta de la importancia que ha tomado este tema y la necesidad de seguir profundizando en la investigación desde los actores que participan en este proceso.

Picture: Marcos Stuardo

VIII SEMINAR:
POVERTY AND INEQUALITY

14th November 2014

Venue: Room 802, Institute of Education, University of London. 20 Bedford Way, London WC1H 0AL

Chair: María Ignacia Arteaga

Programme:

- **Dialogue with Stephen Jenkins, expert in income distribution – London School of Economics.**

- **Jaime Balladares – Institute of Education:**
'Delayed Vocabulary Knowledge, but Age-Appropriate Vocabulary-Learning Mechanisms, in Chilean Pre-Schoolers from Low Socioeconomic Backgrounds'

- **Margarita Calderon – Lancaster University:**
'Using Participatory Research Methods to Involve and Empower Disadvantaged Chilean Communities in Addressing Literacy'

Questions and answers

- **Claudio Santander – University of York:**
'Inequality and Autonomy'

- **Gabriela Zapata – University of Manchester:**
'Inequality of Opportunity in Chile'

Questions and answers, and final debate about the presentations

Delayed Vocabulary Knowledge, but Age-Appropiate Vocabulary Learning Mechanisms, in Chilean Pre-Schoolers from Low Socioeconomic Backgrounds

JAIME BALLADARES

Vocabulary knowledge is a predictor of language and literacy competence (Lee, 2011).

Children's socioeconomic status (SES) affects their rate of vocabulary acquisition, with children from high SES families exhibiting a broader and richer vocabulary compared to children from low SES families (Arriaga, et al, 1999). The majority of research on this topic has investigated factors related to input and interaction that might explain these differences, e.g. maternal speech (Hoff, 2003) and parental education (Richels, et al, 2013). In contrast, few studies have compared the cognitive mechanisms underlying vocabulary acquisition in children from high and low SES families, even though doing so could have pedagogical implications.

Our hypothesis is that measures of vocabulary knowledge, which relies on input and interactional factors, are affected by SES, but the cognitive skills that underlie vocabulary acquisition are not.

Chile has some of the world's biggest SES disparities in educational performance. Our study investigated vocabulary knowledge and cognitive skills in 125 Chilean preschool children, mean age 60 months (5 SD), split into two groups according to SES (low, N=65; high, N=60). To assess vocabulary knowledge we administered a receptive vocabulary test (PPVT) and a semantic fluency test (category 'animals'). Cognitive skills were evaluated through analogical reasoning – AR (verbal and non-verbal), categorical flexibility, and causal reasoning tasks.

Results show that SES affected these tasks differentially, as predicted. There was a significant effect of SES for receptive vocabulary ($p<.001$) and semantic fluency ($p<.001$). In contrast, cognitive tasks did not show an effect of SES: AR – verbal ($p =.789$), AR – non-verbal ($p=.462$), categorical flexibility ($p=.862$) and causal reasoning ($p=.736$).

We conclude that although vocabulary knowledge is already affected by SES, the cognitive skills that underlie vocabulary acquisition are not.

References

- *Arriaga, R., Fenson, L., Cronan, T. & Pethick, S. (1999). Scores on the MacArthur communicative development inventory of children from low and middle-income families. Applied Psycholinguistics, 19(2), 209-223.*

- *Hoff, E. (2003). The specificity of environmental influence: socioeconomic status affects early vocabulary development via maternal speech. Child Development, 74(5), 1368–1378.*

- *Lee, J. (2011). Size matters: Early vocabulary as a predictor of language and literacy competence. Applied Psycholinguistics, 32, 69–92.*

- *Richels, C., Johnson, K., Walden, T. & Conture, E. (2013). Socioeconomic status, parental education, vocabulary and language skills of children who stutter. Journal of Communication Disorders, 46(4), 361-374.*

Using Participatory Research Methods to Involve and Empower Disasvantaged Chilean Communities in Addressing Literacy

MARGARITA CALDERÓN

The aim of this research is to explore the use of participatory research methods in order to involve and engage with the participants in the research and in the construction of knowledge. In particular, this presentation explores the school and home literacy practices in economically disadvantaged settings in Chile. This research approaches the study of literacy from a social perspective (Heath, 1983; Street, 1984; Barton & Hamilton, 1998). Given the disadvantaged environment of the participants, this study focused on explaining the role of literacy in disadvantaged environments and to what extent and how the context impacts on literacy practices. A participatory approach was developed to observe home and school of 20 students. Participants in the study were 7 to 10 years old students from two different schools. Both schools are situated in disadvantaged areas of Santiago, the capital of Chile. Participants were interviewed to discuss their practices and perceptions and then visited at home to observe their environment and routines regarding literacy practices. The purpose of using a participatory approach was engaging the participants as agents of their own learning. This study raises the need of consider how the children's understanding about literacy influence their involvement and learning about reading and writing. This study supports the idea that children play an active role in their learning (Rogoff, 1990; Rogoff et al., 2007). Children's experiences and perceptions have an important role in their learning process and in particular in how they develop their reading and writing. Some of the findings include that the participants perceived literacy as expert knowledge, so their own understanding of literacy discourage them to be more empowered in their own learning. By making the participants' aware of the relevance of everyday practices in relation with reading and writing, the participants felt more comfortable and empowered towards their literacy practices. Empowerment towards learning implies giving them more tools to succeed in the demanding school environment. In Chile the literacy resources are limited, this study intend to contribute to promote children's own household capital in their development of reading and writing.

References

- *Barton, D., & Hamilton, M. (2012 [1998]). Local literacies. Reading and writing in context. London, New York: Routledge.*

- *Heath, S. B. (1983). Ways with words : language, life, and work in communities and classrooms. Cambridge Cambridgeshire ; New York: Cambridge University Press.*

- *Rogoff, B. (1990). Apprenticeship in thinking. New York: Oxford University Press.*

- *Rogoff, B., Moore, L., Najafi, B., Dexter, A., Correa-Chávez, M., & Solís, J. (2007). Children's development of cultural repertoires through participation in everyday routines and practices. In J. E. Grusec & P. D. Hastings (Eds.), Handbook of socialization (pp. 490-515). New York, NY: Guilford Press.*

- *Street, B. (1984). Literacy in theory and practice. Cambridge Cambridgeshire; New York: Cambridge University Press.*

Inequality and Autonomy

CLAUDIO SANTANDER

Does Equality matter for persons' plans of life? In this presentation I want to defend the idea that Inequality undermines personal autonomy in contexts of social justice. Individual autonomy has been discussed, at least during the last twenty years, as a crucial concept to legitimate social and political institutions. Firstly, I discuss the conception of personal autonomy defended by the egalitarian liberalism of John Rawls in order to conceptualise the idea of equality of consideration. The rationale behind this conception is that any political arrangement should be made on the grounds on an equal treatment to all those involved in democratic deliberation. Secondly, I expose Honneth's critiques to such an account insofar as Rawls' approach would be insufficient regarding contexts of "social vulnerabilities" such as the lack of equality of opportunities. The distributive inequality and the consideration harms taken together then, show how inequality jeopardises personal autonomy by impairing persons' intellectual, affective and material resources for planning and being able to lead a worthwhile life. By following these arguments, I explore some approaches against inequality and argue that a conception of personal autonomy is not only compatible, but rather co-dependent of an egalitarian conception of social justice.

Inequality of Opportunity in Chile

GABRIELA ZAPATA

This paper estimates inequality of opportunity (IOp) for different groups of the Chilean population for the year 2011, using a non-parametric methodology developed by Checchi and Peragine (2010) based on John Roemer's work. Roemer (1993, 1998) classified the determining factors of an individual's socioeconomic outcomes (income, status, etc.) as "circumstances" and "effort". Circumstances are exogenous aspects such as gender, race, family background, or place of birth, which may affect a person's outcomes. Efforts on the contrary are endogenous and depend on individual choice. Therefore, equality of opportunity requires that income does not depend on circumstance variables. I associate inequality of opportunity with three observed circumstances that are beyond the control of the individual: parents' education, family composition (people with whom the person grew up) and poverty rate of the birthplace. I found that 14.83% of total earning inequality can be attributed to opportunities when using only parents' education as circumstance variable, increasing up to 16.4% when we add the other circumstances. However, more interesting results are found when we split the sample further according to different characteristics and circumstances. In this case we find that inequality of opportunity varies from 9% to more than 41% for different subgroups of the population that share the same life circumstances. The highest inequality of opportunity is estimated for men aged 45-65, which accounts for 41.8% of total inequality followed by women aged 35-45 with an IOp rate of 37.31%. All these measures are considered a lower bound of the true measure of inequality of opportunity since with the variables available it is only possible to capture a part of all circumstances that individuals face.

Note:
This is part of the dissertation for the MSc in Economics and Econometrics, University of Bristol

Summary

IGNACIA ARTEAGA

It is well known that inequality is a pressing issue in Chile, as it is the country with the most unequal income distribution among OECD countries (OCDE, 2014), and the fourth country with the highest proportion of people below the poverty line.
However, the seminar approach was aimed at going beyond from the economic debate regarding the outcomes and challenges of conducting research about inequality, because the debate about inequality concerns the ways in which a community decides to protect, support and cooperate in order to create desirable life projects for everyone. Thus, the organisation of the seminar acknowledged that ethical and political arguments are as relevant as is the discussion about income distribution.

With the focus on both the hard and soft parts of inequality, this seminar was envisioned as a journey that enabled us to visit and to discuss not only the challenges of its measurement in economic studies, but also the embodiment of those inequalities from people in other spheres, such as educational performance and philosophical reflection about the relationship of inequality, autonomy and justice.

Therefore, our guest expert in income distribution, Professor Stephen Jenkins (London School of Economics), introduced the economic discussion. The first part of the seminar paid attention to the Chilean educational system as one of the issues at the centre of the debate about inequality, because the historically uneven quality enforcements have tended to reproduce and even increase inequality gaps in our country.

In this vein, Jaime Balladares has sought to test whether children's socioeconomic status (SES) affects their rate of vocabulary acquisition. However, this PhD student at the Institute of Education, the University of London, was not concerned with interactional factors such as maternal speech and parental education that were previously explored, but with the cognitive mechanisms underlying vocabulary acquisition in children from high and low SES families. Consequently, by assessing the vocabulary knowledge and cognitive

skills of 125 Chilean preschool children split into two groups according to SES (low, N=65; high, N=60), the results show that although SES already affects vocabulary knowledge, the cognitive skills that underlie vocabulary acquisition are not affected by the students' socioeconomic backgrounds.

Margarita Calderón also discussed the use of participatory research methods as a way of engaging with and empowering economically disadvantaged participants in the research on literacy practices. With an approach based on the social perspective, her PhD study focused on explaining the role of literacy in disadvantaged environments and the extent to which and the ways that the context impacts on literacy practices. Twenty participants were interviewed to discuss their practices and perceptions regarding reading and writing, and were then visited at home to observe their environments and routines in terms of literacy practices. This study raised concerns regarding the need to consider how children's understanding of literacy influences their involvement and learning about reading and writing. Some of the findings are that the participants perceived literacy as expert knowledge; thus, their understanding of literacy discouraged them from becoming more empowered in their own learning. By making the participants' aware of the relevance of everyday practices in relation to reading and writing, the participants felt more comfortable and empowered towards their literacy practices.

The second part of the seminar then aimed to open up the scope of the discussion about inequality by linking it to concepts of autonomy and justice. Claudio Santander, who has a PhD in Politics, Economics and Philosophy at York University, explored a philosophical argument regarding the ways in which equality plays a part in an individual's life plans. His argument is that inequality jeopardises personal autonomy by impairing a person's intellectual, affective and material resources for planning and ability to lead a worthwhile life. Continuing this argument, he explored certain approaches against inequality and argued that a conception of personal autonomy is not only compatible, but is also co-dependent with an egalitarian conception of social justice.

Finally, the last presentation aimed to discuss the factors that determine an individual's socioeconomic outcomes, such as income or status. Gabriela Zapata, PhD student of Economics at Manchester University, estimated the inequality of opportunity for different sectors of the Chilean population for the year 2011. The model distinguished between "circumstances" and "effort". Circumstances are exogenous aspects, such as gender, race, family background, or place of birth, which may affect a person's outcomes. Effort, on the other hand, depends on individual choice. Therefore, equality of opportunity requires that income does not depend on circumstantial variables. Using this model, she found that 14.83% of total earning inequality could be attributed to opportunities when using only the parental education as a circumstantial variable, increasing to 16.4% when other circumstances were added. However, more interesting results were found when the sample was split according to characteristics and circumstances. In this case, the findings showed that the inequality of opportunity varied from 9% to more than 41% for different subgroups of the population that shared the same life circumstances. Parental education was the most relevant circumstance, followed by the poverty rate of the birthplace and family composition.

The seminar concluded with the presentation by AndesCraft, a community project that aims to empower indigenous communities in the North of Chile, subsequently inviting all the attendees to a delightful reception where researchers conducting studies regarding Chilean inequality could form new networks and share experiences.

Dalogue with dr. Stephen Jenkins

Stephen Jenkins, who is doctor of Philosophy at the University of York, UK, is currently the Professor of Economic and Social Policy, LSE. His research interests include the analysis of the distribution of income and its redistribution through taxation, social security and the labour market, as well as quantitative research methods for the analysis of income

distribution. His most recent books are Changing Fortunes: Income Mobility and Poverty Dynamics in Britain, published by Oxford University Press in 2011, and The Great Recession and the Distribution of Household Income, co-edited by Stephen P. Jenkins and published by Oxford University Press.

We had thirty minutes for an informal dialogue in which everyone who had a question for Professor Jenkins could stand up and briefly ask it. The first question that started the conversation concerned the nature of inequality and the options that we have as society to effectively address the effects that inequality triggers for people who are at the bottom. The questions from the public included the professor's perspective on the relationship between indebtedness and income inequalities or poverty, and the way in which he measures intergenerational poverty rates, among other enquiries.

Professor Jenkins discussed various issues. In particular, he examined the idea of the inevitability of inequality of income in all modern societies; the way in which social policies can reduce poverty, but at the same time, produce adverse incentives; the relationship between inequality and economic growth and its dependence on the definition of inequality itself; and whether indebtedness is a social problem regarding sustainability rather than an individual problem.

Resumen

PAULINA YAVAR

El seminario abordó importantes temas relacionados al problema de la pobreza y la desigualdad presente en nuestra sociedad. Desde distintas perspectivas se dio curso al análisis de este tema que se constituye como un desafío esencial tanto desde una mirada económica como política y moral. El seminario se dividió en dos partes: en la primera se sostuvo un diálogo con el experto invitado, el académico de LSE Stephen Jenkins. En la segunda parte, expusieron su trabajo los investigadores chilenos Jaime Valladares, Margarita Calderón, Claudio Santander y Gabriela Zapata, estudiantes de doctorado de distintas universidades del Reino Unido.

Stephen Jenkins tiene una extensa trayectoria en análisis en torno a la distribución de la renta y su redistribución a través de los impuestos, la seguridad social y el mercado laboral. Su investigación incluye el trabajo sobre las tendencias en la medición de la desigualdad y la pobreza; movilidad de ingresos y de pobreza dinámica; la oferta de trabajo y la percepción de prestaciones de seguridad social. La conversación con el profesor Jenkins se inició con una pregunta amplia referida a la naturaleza de la desigualdad y si se constituye como algo necesario en nuestro tipo de sociedad, y de ser así con qué tipo de opciones se cuenta. A esto el profesor inició su presentación señalando que más bien la desigualdad resulta inevitable en nuestra sociedad, pero que es posible trabajar para nivelar ciertas cosas. En esta línea, el crecimiento no resultaría necesariamente contrapuesto a generar menores niveles de desigualdad, sino todo lo contrario. Se requieren cada vez más recursos para sostener los esfuerzos orientados a disminuir las desigualdades. A esto siguieron preguntas sobre si el endeudamiento tiene una relación particular con las desigualdades de ingreso y la pobreza, considerando que la sociedad chilena cuenta con altos niveles de endeudamiento dirigido a ámbitos como el consumo y la educación, lo cual para algunos esto una oportunidad mientras que para otros constituye un problema social.

La segunda parte del seminario se inició con la presentación de Jaime Balladares, estudiante de doctorado del departamento de Psicología y Desarrollo humano del Institute of Education. Su investigación resulta de

gran relevancia al contar Chile con una de las mayores disparidades del mundo en rendimiento educativo relacionado según el nivel socioeconómico de los estudiantes. Ésta analiza la relación entre la adquisición del vocabulario de preescolares chilenos y el nivel socio económico. Su estudio compara los mecanismos cognitivos subyacentes a la adquisición del lenguaje de niños de distinto nivel socioeconómico, bajo la hipótesis de que estas habilidades cognitivas que subyacen en la adquisición de vocabulario no son afectados por este factor como sí lo es en definitiva la adquisición de conocimiento del vocabulario basado en factores de interacción. La investigación se realizó con 125 niños preescolares chilenos divididos en dos grupos, uno de niños de nivel socioeconómico bajo y el otro alto. A través de la aplicación de pruebas de vocabulario y fluidez semántica, así como de razonamiento analógico, flexibilidad categórica y razonamiento causal, se llegó a la conclusión de que aunque el conocimiento del vocabulario se ve efectivamente afectado por el nivel socioeconómico de estudiante, las habilidades cognitivas que subyacen en la adquisición de vocabulario no lo están.

A continuación vino la presentación de Margarita Calderón acerca del uso de métodos de investigación participativos para involucrar y empoderar a comunidades de sectores desfavorecidos en la tarea de la alfabetización. El estudio se centró en explicar el papel de la literacidad en entornos desfavorecidos y cómo y en qué medida el contexto impacta sobre prácticas de literacidad. De esta manera, con un enfoque participativo se desarrolló la investigación en las casas y las escuelas de estudiantes de entre 7 a 10 años de edad de dos escuelas diferentes. Los participantes fueron entrevistados para hablar de sus prácticas y percepciones, y luego la investigadora visitó sus casas para observar su entorno y rutinas relacionadas con las prácticas de lectura y escritura. Algunas de las conclusiones de esta investigación son que los participantes perciben la alfabetización como un conocimiento experto, por lo que su propia comprensión de la alfabetización los desalienta a estar más empoderados en su propio aprendizaje. Al hacer que los participantes se tornen más conscientes de la relevancia de las prácticas cotidianas en relación con la lectura y la escritura, sienten más compromiso y poder hacia sus prácticas de alfabetización. En Chile los recursos de alfabetización son limitados, por lo que este estudio tiene la intención de contribuir a promover el capital propio de los hogares de los niños en su desarrollo de la lectura y la escritura.

La siguiente presentación fue la del investigador Claudio Santander, estudiante de doctorado de la universidad de York, quien aborda el tema de la desigualdad desde una perspectiva filosófica preguntándose por la importancia de la equidad para los planes de vida de una persona. A través de un análisis de distintas perspectivas teóricas expone el concepto de la autonomía personal en relación al de desigualdad distributiva, mostrando que la desigualdad pone en peligro la autonomía personal al afectar los recursos intelectuales, afectivos y materiales de las personas, socavando finalmente la posibilidad de la planificación y la capacidad de llevar una vida que "vale la pena". Siguiendo esta línea, el investigador explora algunos enfoques contra la desigualdad y sostiene que una concepción de la autonomía personal es no sólo compatible, sino co-dependiente de una concepción igualitaria de la justicia social.

Finalmente fue el turno de Gabriela Zapata, investigadora de la universidad de Manchester, quien presentó un modelo que estima la desigualdad de oportunidades para distintos grupos de la población, utilizando la metodología no paramétrica desarrollada por Checchi y Peragine (2010), basada en la obra de John Roemer. Roemer clasifica los factores determinantes de los resultados socioeconómicos de un individuo (ingresos, estatus, etc.) como "circunstancias" y "esfuerzo". Las circunstancias son aspectos exógenos tales como el género, la raza, los antecedentes familiares, o el lugar de nacimiento, que pueden afectar los resultados de una persona. Los esfuerzos, por el contrario, dependen de la elección individual. Para este modelo se asocia la desigualdad de oportunidades con tres circunstancias observadas que están más allá del control del individuo: la educación de los padres, la composición familiar (personas con las que la persona creció) y la tasa de pobreza del lugar de origen. Al analizar se observa que 14.83% de la desigualdad total

de ingresos se puede atribuir a las oportunidades cuando usamos sólo la educación de los padres como variable de circunstancia, aumentando hasta el 16,4% cuando agregamos las otras circunstancias. Se concluye que la educación de los padres es la circunstancia más relevante, seguido de la tasa de pobreza de la ciudad natal y luego la composición familiar

Importancia de este seminario

Chile es el país con la la desigualdad de ingresos más alta entre los países miembros de la OCDE (OCDE, 2014). El coeficiente de Gini es de 0,50 siendo la media en la OCDE de 0,31. Por otro lado, Chile ocupa el cuarto lugar entre los 34 países miembros con mayor proporción de pobres.

Razones económicas, éticas y políticas colocan el tema de la desigualdad en el centro del debate en nuestra sociedad. Y la discusión no es meramente económica en torno a la distribución del ingreso, sino que la reflexión tiene que ver de manera fundamental con el contrato social, con la forma de cooperación de los individuos en la sociedad. El fundamento material de la desigualdad es económico, pero su trascendencia ética y política es insoslayable. En el centro de este debate se encuentra el tema del sistema educativo, el cual tiende a perpetuar e incluso aumentar las brechas. Chile cuenta con una de las mayores disparidades en rendimiento educativo relacionado al nivel socioeconómico, presentándose una inmensa brecha en la calidad entre la educación pública y privada. Aquí nuevamente Chile se encuentra como el país con el menor gasto público en los cuatro niveles de educación (pre-primaria, primaria, secundaria y superior), frente a los otros 33 países que son parte de la OCDE.

De esta forma, el que estudiantes de doctorado que cursan sus programas en las mejores universidades del mundo tengan puesta su mirada y compromiso con este tema desde distintas perspectivas resulta de una enorme relevancia. Asimismo, el intercambio de ideas y nuevos aportes que propician instancias como este seminario contribuyen a avanzar en este tema tan relevante para nuestra sociedad.

CHILEGLOBAL SEMINARS UK IN YOUTUBE

00. 20th June 2013: Launch of ChileGlobal Seminars UK. Embassy of Chile in London.

01. 8th October 2013: Urban Studies and Environmental Regulations. UCL. Video available here: http://www.youtube.com/watch?v=XDMuhf2ycHM

02. 14th November 2013: Disasters, Emergency and Reconstruction. UCL. Video available here: http://www.youtube.com/watch?v=rqzJxaWkr48

03. 20th February 2014: Biotechnology and Medical Sciences. UCL. Video available here: http://www.youtube.com/watch?v=GcCJRSEyXcU&feature=youtu.be

04. 6th March 2014: Music. Embassy of Chile in London. Video available here: http://youtu.be/XRM7Rmu6zno

05: 22nd May 2014: Education. Institute of Education, London. Video available here: http://youtu.be/ReTF1CYBP9c

06: 5th June 2014: Applied Technologies in Medical Sciences. UCL. Video available here: http://youtu.be/zvpAyJjtMbA

07. 15th October 2014: English as a Foreign Language in Chile. Institute of Education. Video available here: https://www.youtube.com/watch?v=2dynKEv_iAI

08. 14th November: Poverty and Inequality. Institute of Education. Video available here: https://www.youtube.com/playlist?list=PLraDTBqYpV4j_9aIl1OAYu5hFQtAJ-h1F

00. 20 de Junio, 2013: Lanzamiento de los ChileGlobal Seminars UK. Embajada de Chile en Londres.

01. 8 de Octubre, 2013: Estudios Urbanos y Regulaciones medioambientales. UCL. Video disponible aquí: http://www.youtube.com/watch?v=XDMuhf2ycHM

02. 14 de Noviembre, 2013: Desastres, Emergencia y Reconstrucción. UCL. Video disponible aquí: http://www.youtube.com/watch?v=rqzJxaWkr48

03. 20 de Febrero 2014: Biotecnología y Ciencias Médicas. UCL. Video disponible aquí: http://www.youtube.com/watch?v=GcCJRSEyXcU&feature=youtu.be

04. 6 de Marzo, 2014: Música. Embajada de Chile en Londres. Video disponible aquí: http://youtu.be/XRM7Rmu6zno

05: 22 Mayo 2014: Educación. Institute of Education, Londres. Video disponible aquí: http://youtu.be/ReTF1CYBP9c

06: 5 de Junio 2014: Tecnologías aplicadas a Ciencias Médicas. UCL. Video disponible aquí: http://youtu.be/zvpAyJjtMbA

07. 15 de Octubre 2014. Inglés como segundo idioma en Chile. Institute of Education. Video disponible aquí: https://www.youtube.com/watch?v=2dynKEv_iAI

08. 14 de Noviembre. Pobreza e inequidad. Institute of Education. Video disponible aquí: https://www.youtube.com/playlist?list=PLraDTBqYpV4j_9aIl1OAYu5hFQtAJ-h1F

EDITORS

Elizabeth Wagemann is a trained Architect and conducts research on housing in extreme situations using prefabricated and modular designs. She graduated from Universidad Católica de Chile with a Bachelor of Architecture (2001) and a Master in Architecture (2005). She received an MPhil in Architecture (2012) from the University of Cambridge and is currently a PhD candidate at the same university.

Bernardita Devilat is a trained Architect and Master in Architecture from the Pontificia Universidad Católica de Chile. She has been studying re-construction after earthquakes in Chilean heritage areas since the 2005 earthquake, when she co-founded Tarapacá Project. She taught Architectural Design at her university from 2009 to 2010 and worked subsequently in the re-construction process after the 2010 earthquake at the Ministry of Housing and Urban Development of Chile. She is currently a PhD candidate at The Bartlett School of Architecture, University College London.

Dana Brablec is a Cambridge-based political scientist, researching on the social and political situation of Chilean Mapuche indigenous peoples. She graduated from Pontificia Universidad Católica de Chile with a Bachelor in Political Science (2010) and a MSc in Democracy and Comparative Politics from the University College London, UCL (2013). Dana is a current first year PhD student in Sociology at the University of Cambridge.

Marcos Stuardo is a Chilean London-based composer. He obtained his 'Licenciatura en Composición' (Bachelor in Composition) with the Highest Distinction at Universidad de Chile under the tutelage of Professor Andrés Maupoint. At King's College London he has been studying with Professor Silvina Milstein and was awarded the Master in Music degree (Distinction). Marcos is a current MPhil/PhD student at King's working under the supervision of Silvina.

Cristian Soza is Master in Genetics from Universidad de Chile. He obtained his PhD in science at the Max-Planck Institute of Immunobiology and Epigenetics (Albert-Ludwigs-Universität) Freiburg, Germany, where he studied thymus and T cell development with Professor Thomas Boehm. From 2009 to 2013 he conducted his post-doctoral research on the nature of cellular timing mechanisms and their role in animal development with Dr Julian Lewis and Dr. David Ish-Horowicz at Cancer Research UK in London. He is currently an associate professor at Universidad Andrés Bello and research director at Oncoloop foundation. He is now researching on immune-neuroendocrine modulation during cancer progression.

ORGANISING COMMITTEE CHILEGLOBAL SEMINARS UK

GENERAL COORDINATOR:
Xaviera Gonzalez Wegener
MA Assessment in Education, King's College London
Email: xgonzalezwe@gmail.com

ANTHROPOLOGY:
María Ignacia Arteaga
MPhil/PhD in Anthropology, University College London
Email: ignaciaarteagap@gmail.com

ARCHITECTURE, ART AND DESIGN:
Felipe Lanuza
Architect U. de Chile and Master in Architecture PUC. PhD candidate, The Bartlett School of Architecture, University College London
Email: felipe.lanuza.11@ucl.ac.uk

BIOLOGY AND BIOTECHNOLOGY:
Stephanie Braun
University College London
Email: stephanie.braun.10@ucl.ac.uk
Jessica Ocampos
PhD student. Chemical Engineering & Biotechnology, University of Cambridge
Email: jao37@cam.ac.uk
Ana Quiroga
Imperial College London
Email: a.quiroga-campano12@imperial.ac.uk
Mauricio Zamorano
PhD candidate Biological Systems Engineering Laboratory, Centre for Process System Engineering, Chemical Engineering Department, Imperial College London
Email: m.zamorano11@imperial.ac.uk

BUSINESS, FINANCE AND INDUSTRIAL POLICY:
Carmen Contreras
DPhil Student in International Development, University of Oxford
Email: ccontrerasro@gmail.com

CLIMATE CHANGE AND ENERGY EFFICIENCY:
Pablo Salas
Cambridge Centre for Climate Change Mitigation Research (4CMR) Department of Land Economy University of Cambridge
Email: pas80@cam.ac.uk

COMPUTING:
Stefan Pszczolkowski
Research Assistant, Imperial College London
Email: sp2010@imperial.ac.uk

DISASTERS, EMERGENCIES AND RECONSTRUCTION:

Elizabeth Wagemann
PhD Student, Department of Architecture, University of Cambridge
Email: ecw49@cam.ac.uk
Bernardita Devilat
Architect and Master in Architecture PUC. PhD candidate, The Bartlett School of Architecture, University College London
bernadette.devilat.11@ucl.ac.uk

ECOLOGY:

María Belén Arias
MRes Ecology and Environmental Management, University of York. PhD student, Department of Life Sciences, Imperial College London & Natural History Museum
mba113@imperial.ac.uk

EDUCATION:

Pabla Cornejo Millar
Email: sepacomi2002@yahoo.es
Daniela Figueroa
Institute of Education
MA Leadership
Email: danyfm@gmail.com
Gabriela Báez
Institute of Education
MA Curriculum, Pedagogy and Assessment
Email: gbaezbargellini@ioe.ac.uk
Denise Quiroz
MA Science Education student at Institute of Education
Email: dquirozm@gmail.com
Elizabeth Torrico-Avila
PhD student in Modern Languages University of Southampton
Email: eta2g11@soton.ac.uk

ENGINEERING AND TECHNOLOGY:

Jessica Ocampos
Co Founder at Cambridge Knowledge and Technology Transfer Platform. Director Cambridge Innovation & Enterprise PhD student. Chemical Engineering & Biotechnology, University of Cambridge
Email: jao37@cam.ac.uk

MEDICAL SCIENCES AND PUBLIC HEALTH:

Deborah Navarro
Research Associate & Nutritional Epidemiologist, Universidad: Imperial College London
MSc in Public Health Nutrition, London School of Hygiene and Tropical Medicine
Email: dnavarro.rosenblatt@gmail.com
Sebastián Aguayo
PhD student, Eastman Dental Institute, University College London
Email: sebastian.aguayo.13@ucl.ac.uk

MUSIC:

Marcos Stuardo
MMus King's College London , MPhil/PhD student at King's College London
Email: marcos.stuardo@ug.uchile.cl

Katia Chornik
Post doctorate. Leverhulme Early-Career Fellow. Department of Music University of Manchester
Email: katia.chornik@manchester.ac.uk

PLANNING AND URBAN STUDIES:

Rodrigo Caimanque
PhD candidate at The Bartlett Development Planning Unit University College London
Email: rodrigo.leverone.10@ucl.ac.uk

Francisco Vergara
PhD candidate at The Bartlett Development Planning Unit
MSc in Building and Urban Design in Development,University College London
Email: francisco.vergara.12@gmail.com

POLITICAL SCIENCES AND PUBLIC POLICIES:

Dana Brablec
MSc in Democracy and Comparative Politics, UCL . PhD student in Sociology at the University of Cambridge
Email: dabrable@uc.cl

Alisson Silva
MPA student, London School of Economics and Political Science
Email: A.R.Silva-Lopez@lse.ac.uk

Catalina de la Cruz
MPhil/PhD at The institute of The Americas, University College London
Email: delacruz.pincetti@gmail.com

SOCIOLOGY

Paulina Yavar
Sociologist PUC
Email: paulina.yavar@gmail.com

IN CHILE:

Cristian Soza
Research Director at Oncoloop Foundation. Chile . PhD in Science (Doctor Rerum Naturalium). Albert-Ludwings-University, Freiburg, Germany. MSc in Genetics. U. de Chile.
Email: sozaried@gmail.com

PRESENTERS' AFFILIATION

Andrés Herane
Research Student at the Institute of Psychiatry, King's college London
Email: andres.herane@kcl.ac.uk

Alvaro González
PhD Student at the Department of Curriculum, Pedagogy and Assessment, Institute of Education University of London
Email: agonzalez01@ioe.ac.uk

Claudio Santander Martinez
PhD student, School of Politics, Economics and Philosophy, University of York
Email: cs1007@york.ac.uk

Dr. Cristina Navarrete
National head of H&I Services. Director of British bone marrow registry (BBMR). Scientific/Deputy Director of NHS Cord blood bank

Deborah Navarro
Research Associate & Nutritional Epidemiologist, Universidad: Imperial College London
Email: dnavarro.rosenblatt@gmail.com

Elizabeth Torrico-Ávila
PhD student in Modern Languages University of Southampton
Email: eta2g11@soton.ac.uk

Elizabeth Wagemann
PhD Student, Department of Architecture, University of Cambridge
Email: ecw49@cam.ac.uk

Ernesto Calderón
Musical Director 'Ensamble Transatlántico de Música Chilena'

Francisco Vergara
PhD Candidate, The Bartlett Development Planning Unit, University College London
Email: franciscovergarap@gmail.com

Gabriela Zapata Román
PhD Researcher, Brooks World Poverty Institute, University of Manchester
Email: gabriela.zapataroman@postgrad.manchester.ac.uk

Ignacia Ossul
PhD Student, Development Planning Unit, University College London
Email: ignacia.ossul.11@ucl.ac.uk

Jaime Ballardes Hernandez
PhD student at Psychology and Human Development, Institute of Education, University of London
Email: jaime.balladares@mail.udp.cl

Jessica Ocampos
PhD student. Chemical Engineering & Biotechnology, University of Cambridge
Email: ja037@cam.ac.uk

Jorge Soza-Ried
Research Associate. Lymphocyte Development Group. Medical Research Council (MRC). Clinical Sciences Centre , Imperial College London
Email: jorge.ried@csc.mrc.ac.uk

Juan Sebastián Lama
London School of Economics and Political Science
Email: juanlama@gmail.com

Juan de Dios Oyarzún
PhD Student. Department of Humanities and Social Sciences. Institute of Education, University of London
Email: joyarzun@ioe.ac.uak

Katia Chornik
Post doctorate. Leverhulme Early-Career Fellow. Department of Music University of Manchester
Email: katia.chornik@manchester.ac.uk

Loreto Aliaga-Salas
PhD Student in Education/Language Education at the School of Education University of Leeds
Email: edlas@leeds.ac.uk

Lucas Rios Santana
MA English Language Teaching & Applied Linguistics, King's College London
Email: lucas.rios@kcl.ac.uk

Margarita Calderón
PhD Student in Linguistics, Lancaster University
Email: mmcalder@gmail.com

María Jesús Inostroza
PhD Candidate in Language and Linguistics, University of Sheffield
Email: minostroza1@sheffield.ac.uk

Marigen Narea
PhD Candidate at the Department of Social Policy and Centre for the Analysis of Social Exclusion, London School of Economics and Political Science
Email: m.s.narea-biscupovich@lse.ac.uk

Natalia Torres
PhD student at the School of Education, University of Sheffield.
Email: natorres1@sheffield.ac.uk

Néstor Garza
PhD Student at the department of Land Economy, University of Cambridge.
Email: ng350@cam.ac.uk

Pablo Salas
Cambridge Centre for Climate Change Mitigation Research (4CMR) Department of Land Economy University of Cambridge
Email: pas80@cam.ac.uk

Paola Valencia
Master of Science Built Environment: Environmental Design and Engineering. The Barlett, University College London
Email: paovalenciam1@gmail.com

Pía Tabali
PhD candidate at Centre for Applied Linguistics , University of Warwick
Email: P.C.Tabali-Marin@warwick.ac.uk

Sebastián Aguayo
PhD Student, Division of Biomaterials and Tissue Engineering, Eastman Dental Institute, University College London
Email: Sebastian.aguayo.13@ucl.ac.uk

Vicente Sandoval
PhD candidate Development Planning Unit. Universidad: University College London.
Email: vicente.sandoval.h@gmail.com

Ximena Galdames
PhD student at the Department of Curriculum, Pedagogy and Assessment, Universidad: Institute of Education University of London
Email: xgaldames@ioe.ac.uk

ChileGlobal Seminars UK are financially supported by:

Embassy of Chile

in the United Kingdom

ChileGlobal Seminars UK are being held in collaboration with:

LSESU
Chilean society

www.ingramcontent.com/pod-product-compliance
Ingram Content Group UK Ltd.
Pitfield, Milton Keynes, MK11 3LW, UK
UKHW021653190726
13853UKWH00001B/238

9 789563 583465